# BECOMING WHOLE

Daphne
Publications

**Also by Bud Harris, Ph.D.**

*Radical Hope and the Healing Power of Illness: A Jungian Guide to Exploring the Body, Mind, Spirit Connection to Healing*

*Aging Strong: Living It Forward and Giving It Back*

*The Search for Self and the Search for God*

*Cracking Open: A Memoir of Struggling, Passages, and Transformations*

*Sacred Selfishness: A Guide to Living a Life of Substance*

*The Father Quest: Rediscovering an Elemental Force*

*Resurrecting the Unicorn: Masculinity in the 21st Century*

*The Fire and the Rose: The Wedding of Spirituality and Sexuality*

*Knowing the Questions Living the Answers: A Jungian Guide Through the Paradoxes of Peace, Conflict and Love that Mark a Lifetime*


**Coauthored with Massimilla Harris, Ph.D.:**

*Into the Heart of the Feminine: Facing the Death Mother Archetype to Reclaim Love, Strength, and Vitality*

*Like Gold Through Fire: Understanding the Transforming Power of Suffering*

*The Art of Love: The Craft of Relationships: A Practical Guide for Creating the Loving Relationships We Want*

# BECOMING WHOLE

## A Jungian Guide to Individuation

## DR. BUD HARRIS, PH.D.

DAPHNE PUBLICATIONS • ASHEVILLE, NORTH CAROLINA

BECOMING WHOLE:
A JUNGIAN GUIDE TO INDIVIDUATION
COPYRIGHT © 2016 BY BUD HARRIS

DAPHNE PUBLICATIONS, AN IMPRINT OF SPES, INC.

Library of Congress Control Number: 2016911457
Spes, Inc, Asheville, NC

Harris, Clifton T. Bud
Becoming whole: a Jungian guide to individuation/
ISBN 978-0-692-75428-3  Non-fiction
1. Personal Growth  2. Body, Mind and Spirit  3. Jungian Psychology  4. Spirituality

Interior Layout by Susan Yost

**Author's Note:**

This book comprises the text of two lectures and the seminars that accompanied them. I have presented these workshops and seminars in Asheville, North Carolina and in many other cities in the United States over the last ten years. The book includes the questions I asked to spark the audience's reflections and participation. I have also included the exercises from the seminars as well with the hope that you will find them stimulating and useful. As much as possible, I have maintained the original text of each lecture as it was delivered. I believe this makes the lectures more personal and easier to read and doesn't run the risk of changing any of my implied or intended meaning.

Bud Harris, Ph.D.
Asheville, North Carolina

# Contents

# Introduction

*"As the dream opened with the force of something coming from the distant past, I found myself sitting in the front of a Shoney's Big Boy restaurant. The booth I was in was next to the large front window. While I sipped on my morning coffee, I looked out onto the main street of the town I grew up in. Across the street and the railroad tracks, was the white Presbyterian church my mother had taken me to when I was small and where her funeral service had taken place. Farther down the street were the high school, the bank and the shopping district. The fact that Shoney's still included the words 'Big Boy' in its name placed the setting back in history. As I turned my head and looked across the table from me, I saw a small boy with ruffled brown hair and intense blue-grey eyes. Shocked, I realized that he was a five-year-old version of myself, before tragedy had struck our family. I looked into his eyes and he quietly said, 'What have you done with my life?'"*

These lectures and seminars are part of the answer to that little boy's question. They represent a portion of the path of living and working that I have been following for over four decades. My title: *Becoming Whole: A Jungian Guide to Individuation* reveals the common thread running throughout these lectures and seminars. Professionally, the process of becoming whole is called individuation. Personally, I call it the search for Self and the search for God (or the search for whatever you might like to call the Transcendent). However you designate it, individuation is a path of awakening, transforming, becoming conscious and fully engaged in living, being authentically alive and fulfilling the unique pattern within ourselves.

Part 1 of this book "Individuation: The Promise in Jung's Legacy and Why Our Culture Has Trouble Accepting It" includes the C. G. Jung Memorial Lecture, sponsored by the Jung Society of Washington, D.C. that I was invited to give at the Swiss Embassy on the fiftieth anniversary of Jung's death. I believe that the continuing attraction to Jungian psychology rests on Jung's focus on the healthy personality. It also rests on the paradoxes included in the Jungian perspective. We will explore these paradoxes as we look into Jung's ideas that our suffering and struggles become meaningful parts of our lives when understood and that life's hardships can initiate us into a more profound sense of being and satisfaction. Individuation, the centerpiece of Jung's legacy, is a path that shows us how self-knowledge not only helps us navigate the most difficult encounters with ourselves and life but also becomes the creative force behind expanding our psychic structure and attaining a fulfilled life.

In chapter 1, we will focus on the components of Jung's work that make up the spirit of individuation, which teaches us to see some of our most frustrating characteristics as a source of new life. We will learn how to strengthen our personalities for this work and revitalize the feminine in our own natures and lives. This process frees us from our history and inner conflicts and helps us to live in partnership with the Self and the Divine Energy within us and, ultimately, to make a true contribution to life. In chapter 2, we will invite this process into our lives and explore some of the reasons we have trouble accepting it by examining the following topics: (1) The Quest for Consciousness and Living a Life with Soul, (2) The Path of Individuation and Transformation as the Descent into Life, (3) The Jungian Process: Story, Dreams, Healing and Individuation, (4) Creative Transformation: Love and Wholeness.

In part 2, "A Lifetime of Promise: A Jungian Guide to Discovering the Transformative Power in Complexes," we will discover why the continuing attraction to Jungian psychology rests on Jung's focus on the healthy personality. Suffering and struggle don't have to be pathological. They become meaningful parts of life that, when understood, initiate us into a more profound sense of being and satisfaction. In chapter 3, we will examine why complexes, a central focus in Jung's work, are not signs of pathology unless we insist on repressing them, thus turning them into enemies, or we cannot or have not developed the ego strength to face them.

Jung thought that his work with complexes was so important that he almost named his work "Complex Psychology" instead of Analytical Psychology. Jung viewed complexes as both the energy fields and the building blocks of our psychic structures. Chapter 3 will also help us understand how to realize and integrate complexes so they can become the architecture of a fulfilled life. We will see how, like the stone the builders rejected, our most devilish and frustrating complexes hold the greatest promise for expanding our personalities and our lives. We will also review how when they are repressed and battled against, complexes drain our energy like a chronic disease, souring our relationships with ourselves and everyone around us.

Learning how to face these challenges and unleash their transformative powers renews our energy, reconnects us to its source and enables our transformed complex to become the cornerstone in a more creative life. This chapter will show us how we can strengthen our personality for this work and explore the seven steps in transforming a complex from life-draining to life-empowering. As this process continues, we will also look into how it frees us from our history and inner conflicts and helps us live in partnership with our Self and the Divine within us.

Chapter 4 describes some of the major complexes that influence our lives, personally and culturally. We will also examine how the Self and individuation are trying to work through these complexes. In this chapter, I use stories, dreams and fairytales to help us understand the options of growth or regression, of transformation or destruction, that complexes present to us. In addition, we will carefully look at how we can become aware of our central complexes.

The material that I deal with in these lectures has grown from the experiences of my life—experiences that I am very thankful for.

Of course developing this material has transformed me in more ways than I can explain. I believe that all of our efforts to examine who we are and where we are going in order to heal ourselves and our culture are sacred activities. I hope that you will join me in this work with that same spirit. I must also add that presenting this material and interacting with audiences around the country also transformed me and left me deeply moved by the potentials in the human spirit.

# PART ONE

## INDIVIDUATION:
### The Promise in Jung's Legacy and Why Our Culture Has Trouble Accepting It

*"The meaning of 'whole' or 'wholeness' is to make holy or to heal. The descent into the depths will bring healing. It is the way to the total being, to the treasure which suffering mankind is forever seeking, which is hidden in the place guarded by terrible danger."*

– C. G. JUNG, C. W. VOL. 18, PARA. 270

# Chapter 1 : Lecture

# INDIVIDUATION:
## The Promise in Jung's Legacy and Why
## Our Culture Has Trouble Accepting It

The C. G. Jung Memorial Lecture, sponsored by the Jung Society of Washington, D.C. Presented at the Embassy of Switzerland, June 3, 2011, by Jungian Analyst, Dr. Bud Harris. ©

When I began my reflections in preparation for this lecture I remembered a very poignant letter that Dr. Jung wrote to an English friend late in his life. In this letter Dr. Jung said: "I have failed in my foremost task to open people's eyes to the fact that man has a soul, that there is a buried treasure in the field and that our religion and philosophy are in a lamentable state."

As I thought about this letter and my devotion to over four decades of the Jungian process, several very personal memories that had been long buried by the years and my intense inner work slowly came to the surface—brought up by this topic and the blank sheet of paper in front of me. I remembered a time when I was in my early forties and was beginning one of my so-called crises. During this time I had the following dream.

As the dream opened, with the force of something coming from the distant past, I found myself sitting in the front of a Shoney's Big Boy restaurant. The booth I was in was next to the large front windows. While I sipped my morning coffee, I looked out onto the main street of the town I grew up in. Across the street and the railroad tracks was the white Presbyterian Church my mother had taken me to when I was small and where her funeral service had taken place. Further down the street was the high school, the bank, and the shopping district. And, the fact that Shoney's still included the words "Big Boy" in its name placed us back in history.

As I turned my head and looked across the table from me, I saw a small boy with ruffled brown hair and intense blue-grey eyes. Shocked, I realized that he was a five-year-old version of myself before tragedy had struck our family. When I looked into his eyes he quietly said, "What have you done with my life?"

Before I could answer, I awakened from the dream. As I was musing over the dream, I knew that he hadn't been talking about the surface stuff like going to the office, shopping, dieting, or even making a living for my family. Those sensitive eyes were searching for a more serious answer. That small boy was posing the question to me that life asks of us all. And, that question is not "What is the meaning of my life?" It is "What meaning am I creating with my life?"

The search for the answer to that question has brought me here today. My answer to it is to try to be fully engaged in life, so that I can develop a greater awareness of my reality and the truth of my existence, so that my life will have an evolving purpose, values and a way of being fulfilled. And, I am seeking to be in touch with life's spiritual aspects and the spiritual depths within myself, so that I can be sure that love is the foundation of how I live.

Now, if I have aroused your curiosity enough to get you to ask me how I am pursuing this complicated-sounding task, I would answer by telling you that I am doing my level-best to live C. G. Jung's individuation process. Dr. Jung's individuation process is one of our greatest gifts from the twentieth century. Beyond being a brilliant healer of the body and soul, Jung brought us the use of the imagination and the experiences of creativity and love in a new way.

I can put my answer to you very simply by saying that it was the ideas in Dr. Jung's individuation process that challenged me to become more fully engaged in life. Dr. Jung was strongly convinced that only a full engagement in life can give us the necessary material for reflections that can transform our consciousness. In individuation, reflecting upon a life being lived is meant to teach us more about ourselves, to increase our daily self-awareness, to expand our consciousness, and to guide us in cultivating our capacities to love. Without mincing any words Dr. Jung told a convention of pastors before I was born that we must be willing to take risks and make mistakes. And, that if "we do the wrong thing with all of our hearts we will end up at the right place."

Then, to illustrate this amazing conclusion—that has given me so much comfort over the years—Jung used the example of Saint Paul's conversion from the man Saul—who was persecuting the Christians—to Paul who became one of the founders of the Christian religion. It was Saul's pursuit of his own worst mistake, according to Dr. Jung, that put him on the road to Damascus and the total transformation of his life. And then, Dr. Jung electrified me with his position that our mistakes, neuroses, complexes, addictions, and dysfunctions are more than shameful, negative characteristics that we need to ferret out, overcome or get rid of. He considered these things—that we usually dislike or despise about ourselves—as containers of a divine spark.

At first, they appear as blocks to our full development such as the achievement of our goals or hopes and dreams, including those of having relationships built on love and trust. But within these very blocks are the seeds, even the roadmaps and the energy, that when opened and tapped, lead us to wholeness which means the ability to live as fully as possible.

Dr. Jung's thinking is so radical and challenges us to such a transformative way of life that conventional religious and psychological institutions have rarely dared to try to understand what he is trying to teach us. All too often there is nothing in our intellectual and emotional development that can give us the frame of reference we need to grasp what Jung is trying to teach. It took me years of re-education through study, analysis, and new life experiences to be able to even come up with intelligent questions about individuation. However, Jung's teachings captured my imagination and the longings in my heart and soul over forty years ago, and I have devoted my life to this kind of work.

The path of individuation challenges us to grow and to be full of vitality for the rest of our lives. In a way that is demanding and difficult for us to understand, true growth usually begins with a serious problem, a block in our life, a breakdown or a serious illness, or a general feeling of restlessness that is calling for a change in the basic structure of how we perceive ourselves and life. The questioning eyes of my five-year-old self years ago, looking at me in the landscape of my childhood, was reminding me that I needed to differentiate myself, once again, not only from old attitudes, values, and complexes from my childhood, but also those in my recent past and present, including the ones that have supported my success so far.

The final piece of the journey, my midlife journey, was learning to listen more to my unconscious and its expressions, to discover and integrate disowned parts of myself, and to pursue an ultimate wholeness and balance in my life. The most exciting and frightening part of this journey is that it is one of continuous transformation. This reality means it is difficult at times, and always requires devotion. In addition, it forces us to question our basic assumptions about who we are and what we value, again and again. And, we also have to keep in mind that deep down in our personalities our ego always prefers comfort and safety to transformation.

So, we have to face the unpleasant reality that the pursuit of self-knowledge means we question every aspect of conventional wisdom, of our religion, or lack of religion, our notions of what love is, our approaches to problem-solving, our ideas of peace and the value of struggle, the value of suffering, and the meaning of unhappiness in our lives.

In order to bring my discussion down to earth and help clarify what I am talking about I am going to focus on several aspects of Jung's thinking that have been especially important to me in my personal journey and my practice as a Jungian analyst. And, I want to explain and then discuss with you how developing more inner clarity showed me that my conventional view of reality was a fiction, how it challenged my customary sense of ethics, and led me into considering a new sense of ethics.

## The Spirit of Individuation

Now, I want to begin my discussion of the Spirit of Individuation by telling you a story. One day, a few years ago, a woman named Lisa came in to see me. She sat down and softly said, "I'm tired of struggling. I just want to be happy." As she finished her statement, she was quietly weeping. I had noticed that even in her sadness she was dressed in a way that showed she put care into things.

"Can you tell me more?" I asked. She looked like she was wilting as she began to speak. Her shoulders slumped and I could see the weariness in her body and around her eyes. "I've been married for sixteen years," she said. "I think I love my husband, or at least I used to. But we argue a lot and he doesn't seem to desire me. I don't think he even really sees me anymore. We don't talk. But we have two children and he's not a bad father…I'm just exhausted. We've been to counseling. I've read a stack of books. I said it already. I'm worn out. I'm so depressed. I just want to be normal and happy."

Now, at this point three things are going on inside of me. First, I am deeply touched to hear how Lisa, like so many people in our culture, just wants to be normal and happy. This is such a deep human longing in a society that teaches us that is this is what we should want, and that if we can find it, our lives will work out well. And, secondly, I am aware that I must remember fully who I am. I am a Jungian analyst. In the long run, it is not my purpose to simply alleviate suffering, solve problems or help someone make their life work so they can get on with it, or even to be normal and happy. What I do is more complex than that, and I am given purpose and direction in my life and work by Jung's myth of individuation. All of our situations are unique, and so is every encounter that we have in our consulting rooms. And, thirdly, I have to remind myself to put all of my Jungian theory and clinical training aside and to follow Jung's advice, that he states so elegantly in *Memories, Dreams, Reflections*—which is to listen to Lisa's story until I understand what it is like to be in her shoes. This point is fundamental in Jung's approach. Eventually, I am able to understand the true depth of her story because I have worked carefully and reflectively on understanding my own story and continue to do so.

By working with so many people I have learned to be clear on a few points every time I embark with a new person. To begin with, individuation is not a self-improvement program. It is much more than firming up, losing weight, having more positive thoughts, or solving problems and getting on with your life.

And, individuation is not self-actualization. The mythologist Joseph Campbell noted that self-actualization is for people with nothing better to do—people who don't know their personal myth or deeper purpose in life. The humanistic psychologist Abraham Maslow's hierarchy of needs for security, prestige, self-development and even personal relationships are not the primary values a person inspired by their deeper Self, or the thread of their individuation, lives for.

Simply put, individuation is about transformation. It means being willing to embrace a lifetime of full-fledged metamorphosis analogous to a caterpillar becoming a butterfly over and over again. It means letting go of the defining characteristics that make up our identity for the sake of becoming something further enhanced by the Self, with a capital "S", the Divine spark within us. The pain in this process is the pain of breaking through our own limitations. The joy is our increased capacity for living and feeling at home within ourselves, and experiencing our wholeness.

Now, you can very well imagine that when Lisa begins this path, she will probably be accused of becoming self-absorbed by her husband or other friends and family, who find that the way she is relating to them is changing. They may accuse her of becoming selfish and irresponsible. As Lisa develops self-awareness, she may also realize that like many of us, she carries her responsibilities as a burden or a weight. When she does this, like many of us, she is using them in a selfish way, as a defense against looking more closely at herself. This kind of approach will diminish her capacities for growth and eventually make her feel resentful of the people she feels responsible for.

Now, this realization about how we often carry our responsibilities as a burden and a defense is a very important insight. It can be life changing for many of us, so let me repeat it. As Lisa develops self-awareness, she may also realize that, like most of us, she carries her responsibilities in a selfish way—as a burden, a weight, an obstacle against self-examination. Using her responsibilities as a defense mechanism and even as an avoidance of self-love diminishes her and makes her feel resentful of the people she feels responsible for.

However, knowing what I know about the process of individuation gives me hope for Lisa. For example, Lisa tries hard. She has worked at her marriage, and gone to counseling. She argues with her husband and pays attention to how she looks. In addition, she pays attention to her suffering and frustration and tries to do something about it. In other words, Lisa is engaged in life. And, one of our primary goals in facilitating individuation is to get people more fully engaged in life.

Dr. Jung explains clearly that we cannot know how to live our lives in advance; that knowledge can only come as a result of being fully engaged in living. To explain this point he continues his discussion of Saul's conversion to Paul that I mentioned earlier. Jung says, "Saul owed his conversion neither to true love, not to true faith, not to any other truth. It was solely his hatred of the Christians that set him on the road to Damascus and to that decisive experience which was to alter the whole course of his life. He was brought to this experience by following out, with conviction, his own worst mistake." Now, this is no small conclusion to get your head around.

In Lisa's case, for years, whether she has been moved by love or desperation, she is still pursuing something—and this desire on her part gives me hope. And, here's something else that gives me hope for Lisa. As wonderful as all of the benefits of individuation sound, neither I nor anyone I know, chose this path because of its benefits. In fact, we are chosen for it, by something deep within us. And, our awakening—the crack in the illusion of how we are living—our call, generally comes in the form of a personal crisis that lasts, repeats, or gets worse until we begin to answer the call or repress it with such force that it becomes a serious set of emotional or physical symptoms, and we end up in lives that are spiritually and emotionally congealed.

Another aspect of individuation that can bring hope to Lisa is to realize that she hasn't been doing things wrong. We are all too familiar with how our culture hammers us with the idea that if we aren't happy, we aren't getting things right. This insidious pressure made Lisa feel guilty and ashamed. In fact, she felt like a failure in many ways. And most of us have felt the same way at one time or another. These feelings bring us face-to-face with the reality that being normal doesn't mean being happy or fulfilled. In fact, from the standpoint of individuation, we do not want to return to being normal—we want to grow beyond normal.

Lisa's unhappiness, frustrations or symptoms mean that she is facing a psychological and spiritual turning point. Her challenge is to begin a process of transformation that, while difficult in its appearance, will offer great rewards. Lisa, like so many of us in these kinds of situations, also realized deep in her heart that following any other course would ultimately diminish or be destructive to her.

It took some work for Lisa to develop the strength to shift her perspective away from the idea that she must be doing something wrong, or that something was wrong with her if she was suffering so much. It took even more strength and support from me—support grounded in my own personal experience of individuation—to begin to think of her problems as potential teachers, or in other words, guides to transformation and a larger capacity for life.

It is no small task to learn to see our depression, anxiety, weight, relationship problems, addictions, and illnesses as efforts of our psyche to heal us—as symptoms that are trying to get us to change, in ways that will help our lives become better on a more profound level. Jung calls learning to value our problems and how they can lead us into becoming transformed, the "teleological aspects" of symptoms.

As Lisa became brave enough to accept this point of view, she could see that behind her problems and dissatisfactions were hidden the powerful psychological and spiritual influences that had shaped her attitudes toward life, and that had become her guiding principles.

Now, once again speaking as an analyst, let me be clear when I say that if we need to cure, fight, defeat or overcome a symptom or even an illness, we have made our problem into an enemy and are losing the teleological value of it. Of course, it is easy to see that this point of view is counter-cultural. It negates our ideas of control, rationality, curing, and to some extent the notion of alleviating human misery. But if, for example, Lisa makes an enemy of her current feelings of depression, she gives them power. The 43rd hexagram in the *I Ching* helps explain how this process actually works. The hexagram says that, "If evil is branded, it thinks of weapons, and if we do it the favor of fighting against it blow for blow, we lose in the end because then we ourselves get entangled in the hatred and passion." Or, in other words, our traditional approach to dealing with symptoms and problems can easily cause us to develop a war within ourselves.

On the other hand, when Lisa takes the Jungian position, she immediately gains a certain amount of distance and separation from her depression. It becomes what we call something that is "Not-I." This opens a number of doors as to how she can relate to it—as to how to seek to understand it from the inside—and how it may want her to change her life in order to become more whole and complete as a person.

We all know that there is a lot of emphasis on choices in our society. So at one point in our work together, Lisa wondered if better parenting or counseling earlier in her life could have put her on a more satisfying path. During this discussion I shared some of my own experience of growth and how as a businessman my depression made me question my choice of career. Yet it was my experiences during this career that helped me develop the ego strength and maturity to risk further changes and pursue new dreams. It is important to remember that we never know the innermost truth about how our mistakes, failures, and tragedies may be affecting our destinies. Lisa learned quickly and was relieved to discover that we rarely make the wrong choices. We make the ones necessary for our growth and that is what she had done.

In summary, until this point I have been talking about the spirit of individuation. Theoretically, individuation is the conscious realization of our unique personality, including its strengths and weaknesses—and the living with this complexity which makes us a unique and differentiated person. On the personal level, however, it is encountering the difficulties that make us slow down and listen to life. It means beginning the inner journey, accepting the importance of self-knowledge and the unconscious, as a partner in informing our lives. This journey shifts how we look at our inner selves, and the life around us, as we realize that being fully human is a much more profound activity than self-improvement or self-actualization. I have learned that Individuation brings healing as it initiates us into becoming artists of living—people struggling to hold their clarity of vision against the rat-race of busyness and obligations pressing on us today.

## Living the Questions

About midway through our work Lisa commented, "As I look back, I can see how restless I have been, how frustrated, and how hard I was trying to deny it because life seemed so good. Now I realize I was searching. During the first part of our work, I thought I was searching for intimacy and a sense of being loved. Then I began to understand I was searching for much more than that. I needed to discover the path that is my life."

Like myself, Lisa had been caught in the familiar paradox of seeming to have a good life, or a secure life, and yet knowing it wasn't working for her. A dream that Lisa had, in which she was confronted by a furious geisha, had scared her and made her think that something was wrong deep inside of her. As many of you know, dreams themselves are a creative response to our reality and often provide good advice. In Lisa's case, it was this dream that led her to see me. Having a good life and realizing it wasn't working was Lisa's initiation into one of the first tests of awakening consciousness—that of living in a contradiction. It took me an awfully long time to realize that life is made up of living in contradictions. The reality was they scared me, made me anxious and uncomfortable. So I did what most of us do. I denied and repressed the conflicts they caused me.

Just like Lisa, if I had a good life that didn't seem to work for me, did I want to risk it to look for something else? Unfortunately, denial and repression led me to live in a make-believe world that was diminishing me as a person. Living in contradictions is what Jung refers to as living in "the tension of opposites." And, as I have said, we hate to live in contradictions, or in Jung's words, to hold "the tension of opposites." Lisa was afraid her ambivalence about her "good life" would make her look weak and selfish to the people around her. At a deeper level she was afraid that the tension might cause her to do something drastic, something that might hurt the people she loved, disgrace her, or embarrass her family, or eventually break her heart.

However, I have learned that the Jungian approach to these dilemmas can become a springboard into a whole new life. Jung's idea is that if we have the courage to develop the characteristics of, and the arguments for, each side of the contradiction—which means to bring each opposite pole into full conscious awareness— and then hold these two in full consciousness—then the tension between these opposing perspectives will become a source of new creative energy in the unconscious that will give us a solution that is beyond what we could have figured out rationally. Jung labeled this process "the transcendent function."

I know that the first generation Jungian analyst Erich Neumann is right when he says that it is the building up and holding the tensions, that arouses the creative potential in our deepest being. In my experience, these contradictions or conflicts generally arise from two sources. First, the path of our individuation will bring us into conflict with one of our conventional values—a value we have used to help define ourselves or a responsibility or obligation we feel. The second conflict comes when we meet a part of ourselves that we have repressed into our shadow that once again, if accepted, will cause us to change who we think we are.

For example, Lisa, like most of us, started in early childhood to make choices about who she would be and how she would respond to life in ways that would make her feel safe and affirmed. In making these decisions, which were generally made unconsciously while she was growing up, she reduced a situation of conflict by deciding to adopt certain characteristics and cut off other ones. When she decided to win approval, she cut off the prospect of confronting people. When she decided to be rational, she cut away the possibility of becoming furious. When her early life was threatening and she decided to protect herself with a hard emotional shell, she cut away and buried her vulnerability. She cut these things out of her ego-identity and repressed them into her shadow.

This is how we generally develop in the first half of life. The better I am at adapting, the better I am at cutting away opposing thoughts, feelings, and characteristics that might get me in trouble or into a conflict. At some level, we want our lives to be problem and conflict-free in order to function smoothly and feel safe.

The process of growing up and adapting leaves us with an ego that is made up of the things we identified with, for one reason or another, either through adaptation, rebellion, or a refusal to grow up. We then believe we know what we want, what we believe, what we think we can do, what we believe we love, what we believe we value and what we regard as the aim of our lives. Because of the way our environment affected us as we developed, because of the ways we experienced love, and learned instinctively to expect the world to be safe and supportive, or hostile and isolating, and because of other ways we were wounded or affirmed—we found ourselves having to adapt. And that adaptation shaped us, in a one-sided way, as we had to repress parts of ourselves, in order to try and feel a sense of safety and security.

As Lisa and I slowly explored her story and the conflicts she was having, she quickly began to see how helpful, what Jung called the compensatory perspective of the unconscious, is in giving us balance and clarity. In other words, the characters and stories in her dreams, her conflicts, her longings, and yes, even her unhappiness and depression, were giving us clues to the parts of herself that needed to be recognized, reclaimed from her shadow and integrated into her personality, in order for her to become a more authentic person.

It is important that we realize that if we refuse to recognize the help and assistance from our unconscious and rigidly live out of our ego alone, we will be living in a state of continuous error in how we understand ourselves and perceive our lives. We will be wrong about how we understand our relationships and the nature of the world—no matter how successful our lives appear to be. But when our unconscious begins to urge us toward wholeness around mid-life, sometimes sooner, sometimes later, the characteristics and potentials we have repressed or denied seem to be coming back to haunt us. As these parts of ourselves are struggling to emerge, they threaten our idea of how we have defined ourselves, and thrust us into the need to change who we are, how we live—and into the contradictions this necessity brings.

Now, it doesn't take much insight to see that if we don't open our consciousness—our egos—to this growth we will force our denied conflicts out into the world around us and project our shadow characteristics onto our partners, our children, and others, or we will force them into our bodies as physical problems. Repressed shadow conflicts easily become physical problems. This needed opening of our personality takes courage because we must lower the psychological defenses that give us our sense of security and safety, in order to incarnate a greater sense of conscious wholeness.

For example, it took great courage for Lisa to deconstruct the illusion of what she wanted her marriage to be, and yet she found this gave her a new freedom within it. What this meant in terms of individuation was that she held the tension between her ideals of marriage and what she thought she needed, and the reality as she saw it, without acting in ways to damage or abolish either perspective until she found that something new—a new perspective—a new vision of relationships or a new sense of who she was, had evolved in her. She held the tension. She didn't seek to get her ideals or needs met in a new relationship or to sublimate them in an affair, a new house, vacation home, or a great vacation.

Now, again, pay close attention to what I am saying because this is very important. Here is the formula for activating the transcendent function:

1. **Fully engage in life.** In other words, quit seeing life as something we want to avoid. By this I mean, accept that taking risks, loneliness, conflict, defeat, and suffering are not only vital parts of life, they are necessary to transformation, wholeness, and the experience of joy.

2. **Reflect upon your life.** This means to be aware of the contradictions that come up in your life, don't repress them. Amplify and explore them. Make the opposites fully conscious and hold them in your awareness. Use your journal, dreams, and active imagination to help you in the way I explain in my book, *Sacred Selfishness.*

3. **Bear the burden of the conflict.** Remember that Jung points out that suffering isn't pathological; it is part of life. It is our refusal to bear legitimate suffering that causes neurotic pain. So, don't resort to fight or flight, taking an easy way out, or trying to sublimate or repress the conflict.

4. **Live the transformation.** Remember, we must change the way we live so that our lives are an expression of our expanded consciousness, self-awareness, and purpose. If we don't, all this work has simply been a mind game.

So, remember these four steps: (1) Fully engage in life, (2) Reflect upon your life, (3) Bear the burden of your conflict, and (4) Live the transformation.

Now let's see what this process meant for Lisa. As part of her journey, she had to go through the difficult process of figuring out that what she longed for and wanted in her marriage was an ego ideal based on her history, wounds, and family and cultural values. This doesn't mean what she wanted was wrong. It simply meant that what she was seeking wasn't complete and wasn't based on her potentials for wholeness. Then, as a result of holding the tension, using it to fuel her inner search, reflecting on and amplifying her feelings around the situation, a new solution emerged that we could not have planned or foreseen.

So, it is important to note that Lisa did not simply try to adjust to the "so-called" reality of her situation. Nor did she assume she had to accept her husband for who he was, and suppose that she had no right to ask him to change. What happened is that she discovered a new freedom. By becoming free of her ideal of what a marriage should be, she no longer had to try to make her life work to fit it. She became more authentic and grounded in her own personhood. From this foundation, she could love and relate to her husband and herself in new and evolving ways. I might also mention that if she had decided to leave the relationship due to this new knowledge, she would not have ended up pursuing the same old ideal unconsciously in new relationships.

These experiences of renewal are very satisfying and even bring a sense of wonder. But, they may also put us into a painful paradox. This paradox causes a huge conflict in people that begin the journey with the secret hope of living a beautiful, self-actualized life that has seemed to be constantly eluding them. In my own case, I felt that life had been continually throwing roadblocks in my way. The result was that I wanted to live an "ego-ideal," a vision of life that was actually a fantasy. It was a fantasy that had evolved in compensation for my earlier woundings and longings. My Self, which I was totally out of touch with, when I was that age, had a different story altogether in mind for me. I still had more to learn from the failure of my so-called, at the time, "dreams and ambitions." And so did Lisa.

After several years of work, Lisa had a particularly angry and bitter confrontation with her parents, who were now in their seventies. She was deeply hurt as she was reminded that they had little interest in who she really was, or was becoming. She remarked that she had thought this kind of suffering was in her past.

The reality is that our suffering and its effects can never be fully locked away in the basement of the past. Individuation, however, teaches us how to integrate sorrow, disappointment, illness, and tragedy into a life being fully engaged in. As we follow the path of individuation, we find out that Dr. Jung is showing us how to discover a new blueprint for our lives designed by our deepest Self and not by everyone else. That is why individuation leads us to a more intense feeling of being alive and an awareness of transcendent movements taking place within our selves and in our lives. We will see what these experiences meant to Lisa.

During her next visit Lisa said, "I've been thinking about our discussion of suffering. And, I remember that when I first came to see you I wanted to learn how to find some peace in my life. I thought peace was a lack of conflict or suffering. Now it seems that to be fully alive means being at peace with the idea that life is full of conflict and suffering. Maybe that's what the 'peace that passeth understanding' really is." Lisa is right. Individuation, which is also the art of living or living creatively, means we must develop a new version of our ideas of peace and well-being.

The creativity of life, of the Self, or individuation, always grows out of conflicts, tension and suffering. This is another idea that our culture has trouble understanding and is very resistant to. The archetypal pattern we grow by, is that of transformation which is symbolized by life, death, and rebirth. Our personality experiences the death process of old aspects of ourselves through tension, conflict, betrayal, and destruction—tension between our deep values and conventional values or obligations, being betrayed by our most idealized people and institutions, having conflict within ourselves and with others over these tensions, and finally, the destruction of our fantasies and ideas of how things should be or what we want. Individuation is a continuous flow of transformation. The peace that is brought on, by the individuation process, is the acceptance of tension and conflict as signs of the life force, the Self at work.

## Finding the Home Within

Now, let me go on to talk about finding the sense of home within ourselves. About midway through her analysis, Lisa came in with a dream that had moved and disturbed her. In the dream she was dressed well, in her professional persona, and she was holding the hand of a ten-year-old girl. She and the little girl entered a large house. In the house they walked up flight after flight of stairs. Finally, at the top, they entered a bedroom that was in extreme disarray. Walking carefully into the room, they slowly opened the door to a closet where they found themselves face to face with an old woman who looked like a dreadful witch. But she was sitting on the closet floor crying and crying. Lisa slowly said to me, "All at once I realized that I don't know what it means to be feminine. Here I am as a child—before my whole psyche got overlaid with a masculine education and values that focused on achievement, competition, getting things done, and being in control of my life. And here shut away somewhere is my feminine soul that I have no contact with."

This dream represented another turning point for Lisa and it illustrates one we must all face in individuation. Dr. Jung reported that he worked for several decades with disturbed and unhappy women. Often those years were frustrating for him, until he realized that he was working on the wound to the archetypal feminine principle in our times, that had been inflicted by the ages of rationalism, science, and technology.

Jung knew very well as he developed this idea of the other within us—the unconscious, the shadow, the anima, the animus—that rather than seeing the other as enlivening and expanding, we have been taught to experience differences and otherness as hostile to our identity and our need to control our lives.

As an archetypal principle, the feminine is beyond definition. In terms of Yin in the Chinese tradition, it is the yielding, dark, moist nature of earthiness, which is also solid and continuing. In terms of passion, we see it in the creative destructiveness of the Hindu goddess Kali, the love affairs of the Greek goddess Aphrodite, and, in another sense, the love of Mary and the wisdom of Sophia. This principle doesn't define either women or men as an archetypal energy, it is present in all of us.

In our time, every one of us has been shaped by the masculine principle as the dominant force in the world we live in. Coming from a world of doing, competitiveness, achievement tests, self-discipline or willpower, and being in control—has turned what Jung thought of as the feminine principle, into something negative—an emotional force that we repress and fear, one that we can't control, don't trust, and have difficulty figuring out how to accept, love, and relate to. Of course, a certain amount of the masculine principle of focused consciousness and activity is necessary to become self-responsible adults. But, if we are limited to only that, our capacities for love, creativity, and connectedness to life are also limited.

In Jung's perspective, receptivity to the creative principle of the Self is necessary for the transformative acts of self-development in individuation. In his great book, *Symbols of Transformation*, the book that caused his separation from Freud, Jung amplifies the importance of the mother archetype in each of us as the foundation for our creative receptivity and the ability to nurture new beginnings in our lives and new wholeness in our personalities. He also points out that this process leads to enormous tension with the world of the ego and the symbolic "father." In fact, he says we must "slay the father" which means symbolically that we must slay the inhibiting influences of practicality, safety, obligations, and conventional wisdom.

The feminine principle affects how we are "being" in life and how we are "being a person" rather than simply existing. Quite naturally, many of us still associate coming into being, or failing to do so, with the woman who took care of us early in life—which means how we were loved, or not loved at the beginning. And that association determines how we relate to our life, and in particular to our unconscious, our inner life. The modern brain researchers, Lewis, Amini, and Lannon say in their book on attachment theory and brain research, *A General Theory of Love*, that—and listen to this—"From birth to death, love is not just the focus of human experience, but also the life force of the mind, determining our moods, stabilizing our body rhythms, and changing the structures of our brains...Love makes us who we are, and who we can become."

Now Jung who, as usual, was ahead of his time often equated the feminine principle with eros, the formative power of life that works through relatedness—through love in its many forms. The archetypal feminine covers a vast world of images, such as the goddesses in every tradition. And every positive image is matched with a negative one. The nurturing figure of the Madonna is matched by the witch in Hansel and Gretel who devours new life. Both are real; both have their place as opposites in our personalities. And if we are going to become whole, we must be aware of these opposite centers of archetypal energy—of how they live within us and of how they affect our lives.

There are three aspects of the feminine element of being in the Jungian approach. The first one is being grounded within one's own nature. The second one is the capacity to then be truly related to another person and to other people. And the third aspect, which is another aspect of eros, is how personally related we are to life. Of course, Jung includes the aspects of inner and outer relatedness as being interdependent when he speaks of eros as the feminine principle.

When we experience ourselves, our being, as rooted in the unconscious and our instinctual lives, we are rooted in what Jung considered the greater feminine principle or the ground within ourselves. Lisa described this place as knowing when she was standing in her own truth. From this being at home within ourselves, an unforced mode of "doing" evolves—one that is inspired.

All of us, no matter who we are, in the pressures of our busy, complicated lives, lose this fundamental relationship to ourselves, again and again. We get caught in false "doing" that isn't rooted in the ground of our being, the Self. False "doing" manufactures a hollow or false sense of identity and accomplishments. It assaults us with formulas for changing and bettering ourselves, that ultimately leaves us feeling diminished, frustrated, or empty, like imposters. At this very point, when we are in enough distress to be open, Jung loved to tell "The Rainmaker Story" which he used to illustrate our journey of return to ourselves. This story is so popular in our circles that you may have heard it before.

In this story, a remote village in China was experiencing a prolonged drought. The fields were parched, the crops were dying and the people were facing starvation. They had done everything they could. They prayed to their ancestors; their priests took the sacred images from their temples and marched them around the parched fields. But no prayers or rituals brought the rain that they so badly needed.

In despair, the villagers pooled their last few resources and sent for a rainmaker from far away. When the little old man arrived, he found the cattle dying and the people in a miserable state. When the people asked him what he wanted, he said only a small hut and a little food and water. He went into the hut, closed the door, and left the people wondering what he was doing.  On the third day, it began to rain. When he emerged, they asked him what he did. "Oh," he replied, "that is very simple. I didn't do anything. I came from an area that was in Tao, in balance. Your area is disturbed, out of balance, and when I came into it, I became disturbed. I retreated to the little hut to meditate, to bring myself back into balance. When I am able to get myself in order, everything around me is set right."

The point is that when we are caught in false "doing" we create a wasteland for ourselves. The rainmaker does not cause the rain. By returning to the feminine principle of being within, he allows the rain to come. This receptive allowing, that isn't trying to achieve and fix things, allows the wasteland to receive nourishment, and as new growth begins, a healthy form of doing will evolve.

As our journey of individuation progresses, we learn that being at home, in the core of ourselves, is the foundation that gives us the security to be with another, and to be in full relationship to life. Being in the core of ourselves removes the fear of being abandoned or overwhelmed by other people in life. The journey of individuation is in this sense a continuous coming home to ourselves that gives us the ongoing courage to face the suffering involved in allowing our buried talents to emerge, and to realize the innate wisdom within us—that can only be forged by the fires of feelings and passion that bring our soul to an inner glow.

If we can realize that, in general, the basic masculine or ego attitude toward life is one of focus, division, accomplishment, and change and the feminine (in either sex) is more nearly one of acceptance, gestation, transformation, the unity of life, and a readiness for relationships—then we can accept a rudimentary division of the psyche into masculine and feminine. To discover what the feminine really means to us personally is to go inward, and look for the images we find in dreams and our creative imagination. There is no formula. Lisa began this quest with active imagination by having continuous dialogs with the witch and herself, as a young girl. She discovered that there is joy in finding what has been lost and in cultivating feelings and potentials that have laid fallow for a lifetime.

As our final session was coming to a close, Lisa leaned forward and said to me, "Looking inward has helped me feel the presence of love in my life. That something has been interested in me all along, guiding my life, supporting it in some strange way—trying to become known by me. It's somewhere within myself. It seems funny I had to seek it, while at the same time allow it to find me. It brings a sense of peace, or serenity, no matter what hardships I have to face." This describes Lisa's experience of what we call the "Self."

I would like to end with a quotation from Jung's closing paragraph in "The Technique of Differentiation" in Volume 7 of *The Collected Works*. Jung says, "Here one may ask, perhaps, why it is so desirable that a man should be individuated. Not only is it desirable, it is absolutely indispensable because through his contamination with others he falls into situations and commits actions that bring him into disharmony with himself. From all states of unconscious contamination and non-differentiation, there is begotten a compulsion to be and to act in a way contrary to one's own nature...For these reasons individuation is indispensable for certain people, not only as a therapeutic necessity, but as a high ideal, an idea of the best we can do. Nor should I omit to remark that it is at the same time the primitive Christian ideal of the Kingdom of Heaven that 'is within you.' The idea at the bottom of this ideal is that right action comes from right thinking, and there is no cure and no improving of the world that does not begin with the individual himself."

I like the ideas in this statement by Dr. Jung and I feel strengthened by knowing that pursuing this inner path, a path of purpose and value, not only brings me personal fulfillment, it brings me into a world where I can make a unique contribution. By being devoted to the individuation process, I have learned that no matter how desperate the moment in history is, I can change my life in the direction of a greater wholeness of being and of experiencing love in a greater awareness of the mystery of love.

After pursuing this path and carefully studying Dr. Jung's work, I am left wondering why it is so hard for our culture to understand that our symptoms and difficulties are trying to transform us. And yet, I also realize that to answer this question we must re-learn that the cultivation of wisdom is more important and of more benefit to our lives than the acquisition of knowledge alone.

---

## Questions to Expand Our Understanding

1. I would like to ask you to write your reflections about Jung's individuation process as a path of awareness.

2. Did anything surprise you in this section?

3. What did you think and feel about the statement that "our symptoms and difficulties are trying to transform us"?

---

## Chapter 2 : Seminar

---

# INDIVIDUATION:
# The Promise in Jung's Legacy and Why
# Our Culture Has Trouble Accepting It

When I opened my lecture, "The Promise in Jung's Legacy and Why Our Culture has Trouble Accepting It," I mentioned a letter that Jung wrote late in his life where he said that he considered his life a failure because he had been unsuccessful in opening people's eyes to the fact that we have a soul and there is a buried treasure in the field—a field and a treasure that we cannot see through the lens of our conventional perspective.

As I continued musing over this letter, I remembered a dream that came during one of my mid-life crises where I was sitting across the table from a five-year-old version of myself. This very serious lad, and indeed I have always been serious, looked me carefully in the eye and asked me, "What have you done with my life?" The search for the answer to that question has brought me here today and my answer has been my devotion to living the individuation process.

During the evening lecture, I mentioned what I believe are some of Jung's most helpful points about living this way. One of my favorites is that, "If you do the wrong thing with all of your heart, you will end up at the right place." In other words, life requires our full engagement, or we have no foundation for developing self-awareness, consciousness, and individuation.

**Questions to Expand Our Understanding**

1.  I wonder what you think of that statement?
2.  What is your emotional response to it?

As I continued, I also explained—and I think this point is a very important one—that all too often there is nothing in our intellectual and emotional development, in our shaping and educational processes, that can give us the frame of reference that we need in order to grasp what Jung is trying to teach. As we grew up, we identified with the dominant cultural complexes in our society. These cultural complexes are the attitudes and perspectives that supply the lens through which we see ourselves and life. For example, in general, our educational systems teach us to accumulate facts, ideas, and concepts that it considers a body of knowledge. On the other hand, individuation teaches us to build our consciousness and our capacities for love by being fully engaged in life, reflecting upon our experiences, and bringing what we have learned into a new version of living. I will say more about this process later, but you can quickly see that individuation is the cultivation of wisdom and receptivity, rather than the building of a body of knowledge.

This process in itself is counter cultural. In a society that values concepts, facts, goals, accomplishing things, focusing on other people, positive thinking, and so on, individuation gives us a new perspective, a new language, and new practices to help us understand the experiences we all have as human beings. These are the experiences of a life where we are fully engaged in it. These experiences need to be cultivated and reflected upon, intentionally and precisely, in order to serve as a force not only for self-knowledge but also for self-transformation.

Through discussing the following topics, I'm going to explain individuation and why we have trouble accepting it:

## I. The Quest for Consciousness and Living a Life with Soul

Living a life with soul and consciousness requires that we give up our roles as victims and create an inner culture of questioning and seeking. Normally we live in a dream state, where our perceptions on the inside are governed by the complexes that control our egos, and on the outside, our reality is the illusion created by the complexes we are projecting. In awakening from this dream state, I think it helpful to consider what I mean when I say, "living a life with soul." Here are a few ideas for us to consider:

**Living a Life of Soul**
1. *Amor Fati* – Love Your Fate
2. New Heroism – A Turning Point
3. Transform From Victim to Seeker
4. Right Relationship with Depth
5. Become a Witness
6. Become an Apprentice
7. Relationship with Unconscious and Self – Our Lifetime's Inner Work

To begin with, Amor Fati means accepting our fate, a term from Nietzsche that both Jung and Campbell were fond of using. This is really a second-half-of-life need—that is, a state of longing for meaning. We are thrust into this state after experiencing the psychological heroism of the first half of life. As you may know, heroism, in the first half of life, describes the quest for independence, identity, and a place in the world. We need this heroic attitude in order to overcome and subdue the dragon of our dependency needs. Heroism supports our struggle to achieve a place in the world and stability in love and work. But when midlife, unhappiness, trauma, or illness thrusts us into the search for meaning—as well as the need for the support of our own depths and the Divine within us, the Self—a new kind of heroism is called for. This heroism is the ability to say yes to our fate, to what is already happening to us, to dive into it and into our own depths.

Such is the transformation Parsifal made when he turned from being a glorious knight—the fulfillment of a childhood dream—into a knight seeking the grail and the right questions to ask of it, in order to bring new vitality and wholeness into the kingdom, which is the symbol of our inner being. It is the turn that Chiron the centaur made when he gave up eternal life and the inflated sense that he could be his own redeemer. He began to cooperate with the forces that shaped him and, at that moment, was transformed from a tragic victim into a courageous seeker, one who was prepared to plunge into the unknown in search of healing, wholeness, authenticity, and a new dynamic spirit of life. By doing this, he became the guiding archetypal spirit of the wounded healer. And incidentally, if we are in pain—whether it is psychological, emotional, or physical—making this turn will lessen it.

## THE RIGHT RELATIONSHIP WITH DEPTH

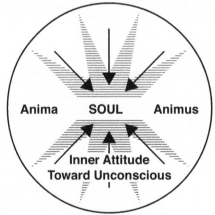

This turning point marks a transition in our lives toward having what we might call a "right relationship" with our depth...and our depth—the Self—will respond to our seeking a relationship with it.

In the spirit of this relationship, we become a *witness* to what wants to unfold in our lives and an *apprentice* to what life, our complexes, our troubles, our failures, and the Self are trying to teach us.

Living with soul, thus, is a transformation of our heroic attitude of winning, achieving, accomplishment, and trying to be in control of our lives, into a new kind of heroism that accepts the reality of where and who we are, and then moves us to become a courageous explorer of the interaction between our inner and outer worlds. And we explore by reflecting upon our experiences...upon how our story has led us to these experiences...and upon how and what our unconscious (including our complexes as well as the Self) is trying to teach us. Whatever our life's work may be in a material sense, this inward journey and our relationship with our unconscious and the Self will be our lifetime's inner work.

## Questions to Expand Our Understanding

Now, I've said a lot. Let us stop for a few questions.

I would like to ask you:

1. What do you think the significance of this turning point is?
2. How do you think it can be relevant to your life right now?

## Dangers in This Process of Turning Inward

...for you to reflect on...

1. Sounding prescriptive and intellectual
2. Making it sound too easy when the emotional side may be deep, profound and challenging
3. Ego takes over—unconscious and Self lose their position as "not I"

## Understanding Our Biggest Danger— The Collective Shadow

1. How it negates inner world and inner journey
2. How it causes us to split ourselves and thus to think we can control everything
3. How it emphasizes our obligations and duties

The biggest danger that we face within and without ourselves is the collective shadow of our culture. Let me tell you a few ways this shadow affects us.

1. We, as a society, have negated the value of the inner world, the inner journey, and the idea of a committed search for the Divine within us. Even people who sincerely want to value the inner journey find it difficult to give adequate time to the process—and this is because we are always caught in the undertow of a cultural tide that idolizes concrete outer activity, busyness, and accomplishments.

2. And we split ourselves by thinking we can control everything through consciousness, meaning in this case, *ego consciousness*, or at the other extreme through magic, currently referred to as manifesting things such as abundance and so on.

In the first case, we have to give up the ideas of many of our cherished dreams and fantasies, which are generally compensatory to our major wounds and complexes. And we have to give up our limited ideas of what a psychology is, and by this I mean our notions that we can gain rational or so-called conscious control over our emotions, moods, attractions, destinies, and so on by making "better choices." Better choices aren't controlled—they come naturally, not even as choices, when we have healed and restructured the inner foundation of who and what we are.

In the second case, we have to learn to understand that our self-help gurus and best-selling authors are so popular, not because they are giving an accessible expression to deeper reality, but because they are presenting what the public, which means most of us, wishes were true. For example, few of them endorse "The Descent" that we will talk about next, that is supported in the wisdom traditions of our great religions. Now, I'm not saying we can't learn a few handy things from these people and books. But, I will say that few of them help us live continually in the deep streams of support and transformation that flow within us, or help us to recognize ourselves as the "Beloved" of the Self, the Divine within.

Now there is a third aspect of the collective shadow we have to confront, and that is the idea of obligations and duties we have, and our fantasies of ourselves as good or bad people, or perhaps both. Note that I said confront, not abandon. The obligations—which in fact we often use as a defense against accepting ourselves, and our ideas of who we are good and bad—offer us the fuel for a struggle that can refine and transform us. In addition, when we go against a cultural norm, Jung informs us that we will experience a degree of guilt that can only be expiated by bringing value back to the culture.

---

### Questions to Expand Our Understanding

So, I've made some strong statements here…

1. What kind of responses, thoughts, and feelings do they bring up in you? And these statements are complicated…

2. How do you understand them or what do you think about them?

---

### A Struggle Between our Values, Obligations, and the Call for Transformation

So, on the inner journey, I—meaning my ego—am challenged again and again. It is challenged to separate from my persona and ideals of who and what I should be. It is called, like Moses, to "set my people free from bondage", to let my enslaved feelings and talents out of the captivity of conventional wisdom and obligations—not to run amok but to begin a psycho-spiritual journey to a new land. Like Abraham, our ego is called by the Self to leave the wisdom and security of the culture, out of the land of the "fathers", out of the manufacture of our cultural idols, appearances, and success, and into a new land of opportunity and miracles.

Then we must meet and confront our wounds and our shadows, walk up to our own Golgotha where our ego will suffer and be transformed. Meeting our wounds means creating the interior space to hold the reality of our experiences—our hopes, joys, terrors, hurts, triumphs, and finally our strength. It means accepting the anger and

*31*

rage that breaks the mold of our denials, and frees us to experience the stages of grief inherent in every life, and in every experience of transformation. Leaving denial means seeing the poor dysfunctional men, women, and criminals within us, and going through the stages of grief from former hurts and events that shamed and diminished us.

Meeting our wounds also means redeeming our anima and animus from their inner primitive state, where they are usually attached to our shadow and its complexes. Then the anima and animus become guides to our soul, and we can discover the support of the Self—discover that something inside of us is caring about us, is confirming us, is unfolding our future, and yet will not rescue us from anything.

**The Soul Contract**
*The Soul Contract: Practices for Pursuing the Journey*
1. Engage
2. Reflect
3. Transform Consciousness
4. Live the Transformation

The Soul Contract begins with our becoming fully engaged in life, and proceeds as we learn a devoted practice of reflecting upon our experiences, until our reflections enlarge and transform our consciousness. Then we must integrate this new level of consciousness into our lives. This is the contract: (1) Engage, (2) Reflect, (3) Transform consciousness and (4) Live the transformation.

*The Map of Stage One in the Individuation Process*

---

### The Map of Stage One in the Individuation Process
1. Freedom from Our Parents
2. Freedom from Our Dependency Needs
3. Transform Major Complexes
4. Freedom from World Parents

---

Now I want to share with you a Map for Stage One in our Individuation Process:

1. Freedom from our parents—our mother and father complexes and the complexes we have internalized from them that define us. Now, please remember that freedom from complexes mean transforming them and being transformed by them, not heroically overcoming them. Also remember that deep in our bones we rarely want to change—but deeper in our souls is a longing to become reconciled with possibilities within us that we may only faintly sense.

2. Freedom from our dependency needs: These include our needs for a soul mate—our need to be loved unconditionally—to be truly accepted, understood, and so on.

3. Transforming our major complexes: These complexes reside in our shadows and are rooted in our parental complexes.

4. Freedom from the world parents: Our Jungian name for the parental influences of the culture on our development, world parent complexes include the following.

   a. More dependency needs, such as depending on the culture to define values and directions
   b. Obligations functioning as defenses and complexes
   c. The definition of a good life
   d. The definition of being religious
   e. Other such complexes we have internalized or been indoctrinated into by the culture

Now, so far we are simply out of Egypt, so to speak, and are beginning the journey to the Promised Land. One may wonder: what is worth this kind of commitment? We will explore the answer to this question and the promises of the journey further in the next three sections.

We must also remember that in this journey we talk a lot about suffering, trauma, and struggling because that is an aspect of life. But, the journey is really about transformation, about realizing the deep strengths of a support within us, about surviving intact, and being able to love and to realize that even while we have been caught in illusions, complexes, and denial—something in our nature is still looking out for us.

**EXPERIENCING THE SUPPORT OF THE SELF**

At this point, the Self is experienced as the support of a hidden hand. Learning how to love—without our efforts at it reflecting needy psychological pursuits, idealistic fantasies, or sentimental hopes—is a success in itself. Whether this love brings a successful relationship or not is another story that concerns our destiny. But, simply being able to love in this way means that some part of being human in us has become vitally alive.

## II. The Path of Individuation and Transformation as the Descent into Life

When I think about the title of this second part of the seminar, "The Path of Individuation and Transformation as the Descent into Life," I always find it interesting, even amusing, that when the newest pied piper for enlightenment is speaking in our town, he or she is usually focusing on how we can achieve peace and joy. Well, no wonder! That is what sells or what creates followings because that is what so many of us think we are longing for.

On the other hand, all of our great religions (and I am not speaking of the pied pipers they also have), those religions that religious scholar Huston Smith calls our wisdom traditions, have a very different emphasis. For example, a rabbi famous in Jewish history lived in a tent pitched next to the walls of Jerusalem because he wanted to be close to the poor. When Prince Siddhartha walked out of his father's palace, he came face to face with poverty, illness, and death. These encounters launched his journey into becoming the Buddha. In Christianity, Jesus says in the gospel of Matthew: "For I have come to call not the righteous but sinners," when he was asked about the people he liked to spend his time with.

Our wisdom traditions tell us that the root meaning of the word salvation means "the way of redemption" or the "way to wholeness." As we follow this line of thinking, we discover that our journey into wholeness, or holiness, in the words of the mystical traditions, begins in a paradoxical way—not by a search for peace and joy—but by acknowledging the grit and grist of life: suffering, illness, death, and our alienation from ourselves and the depth of our own spiritual and psychological capacities. Now, this is a very important point: it is the full acceptance of these aspects of ourselves that initiates our journey into becoming fully human, fully incarnated, and more open to joy.

Of course we all want a good life. And when we encounter life's difficulties we want peace of mind, good relationships, *and* we want to keep our lifestyle and habits—the personalities we are used to. And of course our culture supports this point of view. The culture doesn't see our wounds and difficulties as calls for transformation. It sees them as symptoms to alleviate so we can get back to "normal," which actually means functional in a social way, not a spiritual, psychological, or even a personally fulfilling way.

In addition, most of us want to have a vision of life that is successful, prosperous, and fulfilling, and if we have children, we want to have a dream of a successful life for them. We get angry with them, ourselves, and life when our dreams and visions fail. But, the failures of these dreams and visions are very important for they are meant to awaken us to compassion—compassion not for others, but for ourselves and for how difficult life is.

Generally we need our dreams of a good life to carry us into adulthood. But later, we also need for these dreams to fail, in order to make way for our wholeness to begin to emerge and be discovered. And we need the self-compassion that these experiences can generate, in order to accept the difficulties in our lives as spiritual and psychological incubations and not as failures. Plus, as we begin to do the work in what Jung called "the realization of our shadow," we need this capacity for compassion in order to accept the poor, dispossessed and disapproved parts of ourselves.

To illustrate this point, I'll share with you the words of the Ba'al Shem Tov, founder of the Hassidic tradition in Judaism. He said, "There are many rooms in God's castle." Does that sound familiar? He then went on to say, "There is, however, one key that opens every room, and *that* key is a broken heart."

---

### Questions to Expand Our Understanding

1. How do you feel about the statement of the Ba'al Shem Tov?
2. What do you think about this emphasis on suffering, the disowned, compassion, the broken heart and so on?

---

The statement of the Ba'al Shem Tov reminds us of the emotional reality involved in the realization of our shadow, of making a true descent into life. Here is a chart from Barbara Hannah's book on Jung. Notice the Island of Consciousness above the wave and the Unconscious below the wave.

**EGO AND SHADOW**

Ego, the center of consciousness

Shadow

In this diagram, our ego develops like an island out of our unconscious as the basis of our identity. The ego consists of the things, attitudes, and values we identified with as we grew up in order to form who we are. To function in our families and society, we usually identify with values, attitudes, and behaviors that either bring approval, affirmation, and safety or are instead a desperate rebellion to keep ourselves from being overwhelmed. The opposite of what we identify with goes into our shadow. To illustrate, I have listed virtues and vices on the chart you see here.

| VIRTUES | VICES |
|---------|-------|
| humility | pride |
| generosity | covetousness |
| temperance | lust |
| love | envy |
| moderation | gluttony |
| patience | anger |
| industry | sloth |

## DEALING WITH THE PARADOXES OF OUR SHADOWS

1. Acceptance
2. Valuing

As we develop psychological maturity, the problem we run into is that every virtue can have an unseen negative effect. Humility can make us passive and compliant, and it can cause us to build up an unconscious volcano of resentment or even pride in our virtuous behavior. On the other hand, a vice, such as pride, can have a positive effect, urging us to reach beyond ourselves, and it can even save us from despair.

Once again, you can see paradoxes at work here. What happened as we formed our identities is that we generally identified with characteristics, feelings, ideas, and attitudes that we felt would make our lives work, and they came to represent what we thought were our strengths and best values. In other words, we developed our own unconscious lists of virtues and vices to guide us.

When these identifications begin to fail, people come in to see us professionally, because they have become unhappy, discontent, or were never able to form a workable list and want their suffering to stop.

Now, two things make it possible for our suffering to begin to stop. First is the acceptance of our suffering—remember self-compassion is needed, not self-judgment. Acceptance is the necessary first step in transforming anything psychological, according to Jung. But our next question is, what will our suffering be transformed into? The answer, according to Jung, is not into peace and joy but into true suffering, which means facing the real early wounds within ourselves and the truth of our inner contradictions.

The second thing we must do is to value the inhabitants of our shadows—the parts of ourselves that have been disowned, devalued, rejected, and repressed. This all starts with some of our most negative feelings and self-critical voices.

Let me read to you a piece from the New York Times article on *The Red Book* that explains what I mean.

> "Creating the book also led Jung to reformulate how he worked with clients, as evidenced by an entry Shamdasani found in a self-published book written by a former client, in which she recalls Jung's advice for processing what went on in the deeper and sometimes frightening parts of her mind.
> 'I should advise you to put it all down as beautifully as you can—in some beautifully bound book,' Jung instructed. It will seem as if you were making the visions banal—but then you need to do that—then you are freed from the power of them…. Then when these things are in some precious book you can go to the book and turn over the pages and for you it will be your church—your cathedral—the silent places of your spirit where you will

find renewal. If anyone tells you that it is morbid or neurotic and you listen to them—then you will lose your soul—for in that book is your soul.'"

This is the way Massimilla and I value our own shadows. You might also want to remember that nothing in our shadow frightens us more than our own denied and impoverished potentials.

---

## Questions to Expand Our Understanding

Valuing our negativity? Making it sacred?

1. What do you think of that?

---

In summary, knowing our shadow is to become aware of the parts of our personalities that we have repressed or disassociated from in our development and early adjustment, both good and bad.

### Two Paths to Knowing Our Shadows

---

## Two Paths to Knowing Our Shadows

1. Dreams – same sex people in our dreams

   a. What are your associations with, or to these people, in specific, or in general if you don't know them?

   b. What are they doing in your dream? How are they behaving? What do you think about their character?

   c. Are you attracted by them or repelled by them?

   d. Are you afraid of them, disgusted by them, etc.?

2. Projections

   a. Note the irrational strength of our feeling about someone.

   b. Note our difficulty in getting rid of these feelings, passion, the broken heart and so on.

---

There are two primary paths that we can follow in looking for our shadows. The first one is in dreams. Figures who are the same sex as ourselves represent shadow aspects of ourselves. Let me give you a brief example.

A few days ago, an analysand told me a dream. It had followed a long and somewhat controversial discussion he had the previous evening with his wife. In the dream, he was at a celebration with former President Clinton. When I asked him what his associations were with President Clinton, he said that he considered Clinton a completely political animal. That he could not tell if he truly had any values or not, because he always seemed to be compromising what he said he believed in, for political expediency. As he was talking, his face began to change its expression, as he recognized the dream image in himself, in terms of how he dealt with his wife.

The second pathway to our shadows that we can follow is in projections. The irrational strength of our feelings and our inability to get rid of them alert us to the idea that the projection is our issue, no matter how justified we feel otherwise. The resentments that keep us from going to sleep and the arguments that go on and on in our minds illustrate that projections are at work. In an extreme case, we may see someone who seems to personify all that is shifty, cowardly, or evasive. They will arouse in us dislike, animosity, and even fear. We will find it impossible to be fair with them.

They are unbearable to us because they stand for something within ourselves which we do not wish to own. They enable us to maintain our good opinion of ourselves, because the projections carry our rejected, bad qualities. In some cases, the projections may even carry good qualities—which, otherwise, we might have to acknowledge as our very own qualities.

Getting to know our shadows is a painful journey because we must crucify our own opinions of ourselves. The mystics aptly termed this process the "purification of the Self." Literature and mythology refer to this process as a "descent" that requires faith, courage, and usually a guide.

I think that it is probably apparent at this point that the realization of our shadow compels us to outgrow our parents' psychology, as well as to become aware of and outgrow our society's psychology. Both of these are closely tied in with our shadow—our parents, our parental homes, policemen, institutions, and their representatives often show up in our dreams, in order to help us come to grips with "conventional" attitudes and values we have internalized.

## Detachment

The psychological process of viewing our ego development in relation to our families' and society's psychology, values, and needs is akin to the mystical process called "detachment."

Detachment in the mystical process has several levels:

1. Poverty: This means giving up the things that chain our spirits. In the parable of the "rich young man," it was not his wealth, but his attachment to it, that caused Jesus to admonish him to give it up.

2. Chastity: This means to keep the personality (the soul, in religious terms) open only to the inner voice of the Self, the Divine within.

3. Obedience: This means to follow the razor's edge of the inner voice and to become strengthened and refined by the conflicts between that inner voice and conventional values and wisdom.

The next step for the mystics is *mortification*, which in our Jungian language is the realization of the shadow. Through mortification we bring our old personality into the spirit and form of the new, enlarged one. The interesting point about this kind of work is that it is never over, and it is always enriching. This is true because the more light we create, the more shadow we create.

---

## Questions to Expand Our Understanding

1. Does the process of detachment make sense?

2. Consider this quotation:
   "The less I can say, 'THEY do this, THEY are wrong, THEY must be fought,' the more I become a serious problem to myself."

## III. The Jungian Process: Story, Dreams, Healing and Individuation

In this part of our seminar we are going to look at how important the concept of story is in Jungian psychology, and how important the idea of story—our story and the greater story of humanity... and our knowledge of our story, in particular—is for developing consciousness and for individuation.

In olden times, we created culture by using stories to give a sense of form and meaning to life, to give us a sense of the mysteries of life, and to connect us to those mysteries. Today we tell our children stories to entertain and to teach them. They, in turn, hunger for the archetypal themes in stories that connect them to mysteries. The current popularity of the Percy Jackson books that connect children with the Divine—he is the son of Poseidon and a mortal woman—and to the hero myth, as the characters in the book develop and fight evil, is a good example.

All of our great wisdom traditions and religions are made up of stories that teach. And we are struggling to re-imagine these stories so they can help inform our lives. Many of us have had the experience that when we began a relationship as lovers, our intimacy was initiated as we shared our stories with each other. Stories connect us with each other, with important values, with patterns of living that give meaning and healing, and they connect us with the transcendent aspects of life, as well as our deeper selves. A real story touches the mind, the heart, and the soul.

Yet we are living in a world that is destructive to our experience of stories. Television gives us disconnected news blips, soap operas, sitcoms, and reality shows that have no deeper theme, and everything is fragmented by the insertion of commercials. Talk radio has no story to tell us, as it tries only to arouse emotions. Or movies such as *Avatar* turn archetypal themes into emotional entertainment and rob these themes of their truly transformative power. This cultural direction has caused us to develop a resistance to "story" in its more profound forms. The hum of noise, often referred to as white noise, urges us to want security, the *status quo*, or to want to stop the world and get off. The world supports our resistance to stories, because to pay attention to them takes time.

### Questions for Reflection

1. What is your response is to what I have been saying about the importance of story?

2. What are your thoughts about our challenges in this culture to "story" in its more profound forms?

I began my Jungian experience in the same way that many people have, by reading Jung's autobiography, *Memories, Dreams, Reflections*. Every time I've re-read this book, and I've done so many times, I am struck in my own inner work and in my professional work when Jung writes, on page 117, "…the patient who comes to us has a story that is not told and which, as a rule, no one knows of. To my mind, therapy only really begins after the investigation of that wholly personal story. It is the patient's secret, the rock against which he [or she] is shattered."

Dr. Jung continues, "…the problem is always the whole person, never the symptom alone. We must ask questions which challenge the whole personality." In other words, symptoms arise from this blockage of our story, and we must discover this story in order to have our life follow a track of authenticity, meaning, and fulfillment.

Of course, every time I read this passage, I wonder anew what story I am living, is it my real story or is it a cover story that protects me, helps me fit in, and makes my life look like it's working?

### Questions for Reflection

1. Am I living in my story?

2. Am I living a cover story?

3. How has this idea of Jung affected you?

4. What feelings came up when I said we have a secret story?

5. What feelings came up when I said that it may be the rock that blocks you or shatters your hopes and dreams?

## Dreams and Story

---

**Every dream is or has a story behind it.**
**Every complex has a story behind it.**

---

Now I would like to talk about the importance of "story" in our dreams. In Jungian psychology every dream is a story, or has a story behind it. And in addition, as we shall see later, every complex has a story behind it, as well. In order to understand a dream, we try to understand its story and what it is like for us and the characters in the dream, to be in that particular story. So, as we look at dreams we look at Classic Dream Structure.

---

### Classic Dream Structure:

1. The opening place and situation, the beginning;

2. The complications, the flow of action, the complications that occur, or the lack of action;

3. The climax of the action, the situation that is a turning point;

4. And finally we look at the result, what has been solved, pointed out or left unsolved.

---

In other words, we look at the dream from the standpoint of a classic, dramatic structure. This perspective, the dream as a story, helps its flow of events make sense. For example, the dream opens and I am in my childhood home. As I write my associations to the dream, I will write about what it felt like to be in my childhood home, and I will wonder why or how I am still in this boyhood situation.

As I go through my dream this way, one sentence or image at a time, I will be amplifying the dream into a broader story, and I will also become more personally informed by its story. Dreams remind us to pay attention to the story of our lives, and they connect us to this story. Dreams with shadow figures in them are telling us stories about our identities. Dreams with anima or animus figures are telling us stories about our relationships to ourselves and others. Dreams with archetypal images in them speak about destiny, transformation, deep healing, and other soul issues. And, if we develop almost every dream sufficiently, we will usually come to a deeper theme, an archetypal pattern.

## Questions for Reflection

1. Do you have any thoughts or questions to journal about as you consider dreams as story for you?

2. Have you had dreams that reminded you to pay attention to the story of your life?

### Complexes and Story

Every complex has a story as well…When we know enough about them, complexes, too, can be put into a story form. In Chapter Three, we will go into more detail about complexes. In short, a complex situation looks like this:

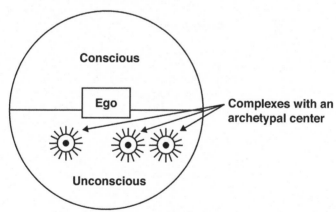

When we face an outer situation that activates a complex, it takes over the decision-making power of our ego. The complex is an energy center with an archetypal core, which means our ego can rarely overcome the energetic power of the archetype with insight and/or willpower.

For example, if I had a non-nurturing mother, in times of stress my negative mother complex will be constellated and I will crave sweets. The complex overrides the ego and says, "I will have what I need—sweets."

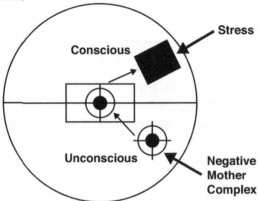

The ego may say no, but the power of the negative complex is stronger.

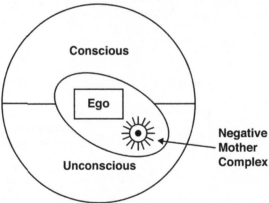

What we must do is accept the complex, and begin an interaction with it that unfolds its story. By following the seven steps I will outline, this interaction with the complex enlarges and strengthens the ego and then the complex becomes transformed, as we uncover and experience the positive side of the archetype. In this case, we reveal and release our capacity to be self-nurturing in a deep sense.

## Life As Story

If we live life as in a story, then we must remember that our childhood is not something that was simply good or wounding, but rather it is the beginning of our story. In that regard, it is like a wellspring that we go back to, not as a source of pathology, but as a source of new life. Our soul-self is our full being: body, mind, spirit, symptoms, fear, love, hurt, expectations, dreams, and fantasy. Many of our problems come when our ego gets scared and tries to use power to repress and overrule the biddings of our instincts and the desires of our hearts, or to hide from powerful emotions like fear, shame, and rage.

Remember that life as story is easier for our ego to comprehend because our flow of experiences can be seen in the context of a form, a "structure" that helps make sense of them. It is the limiting or blockage of our personal stories by ourselves, others, our culture, and the nature of our environment that has tragic consequences. Our symptoms—physical and emotional—can show us how our story is limited. The question then becomes, "Can we change our story, our fate?" The answer is yes. Here are the following seven steps I want to share with you for changing your story.

---

### 7 STEPS for Changing Your Story

1. Make your wounds sacred.
2. Step out of the culture's plot.
3. Allow a new story to emerge.
4. Participate consciously in your story—become a full actor in it.
5. Accept the creative cycle of life: life—death—rebirth.
6. Follow the soul-contract.
7. Realize the story changes because new influences have come to bear on it.

---

## Wounds as Sacred

The first thing we must do is accept our wounds and the complexes they caused, and make them sacred by letting our old stories around them die, so they can become the vehicles through which new stories can emerge.

### Beyond Culture's Plot
Then, we must step out of the limitations imposed on our stories—by the conventional wisdom of our families and society as well as the fear and shame these groups use to limit us.

### Let New Story Emerge
We must, then, be willing to hold the tension and endure the anxiety while a new story is trying to emerge.

### Participate as Full Actor
We must help this emergence by participating consciously, by becoming a full actor in our story.

### Accept Creative Cycle
And, we must remember the importance of accepting the cycle of life, death, and rebirth...and realize that we usually experience the death aspect as conflict, betrayal, and disappointment. This process of accepting the full creative cycle is countercultural in a society that sells the "good life."

### Follow Soul Contract
Our vehicle for building consciousness and fueling transformation is the soul-contract and the practices for pursuing the journey, that I discussed earlier:
1. Engage
2. Reflect
3. Transform consciousness
4. Live the transformation

### Realize New Influences
And, finally, we must trust that our story will change because new influences come to bear on it.

This whole process of Life as Story becomes healing and flows into our ongoing individuation process. We are then in our own unique story of self-realization and the expression of the potential person we are meant to be. For all of this to happen, our ego must become a committed seeker—or we will continue to be caught in a story that never evolves and is unable to fully engage in the love and fullness of life.

What I have been telling you is a real distillation of Jungian theory and very counter-cultural.

---

### Questions to Expand Our Understanding

1. What questions come up for you as you look as the possibility of changing your story?

---

## IV. Creative Transformation, Love, and Wholeness

As we come to this final section of this seminar, I have said in many ways that I am teaching and Jung is teaching us how to have a profound regard for discovering, nourishing, and preserving our relationship with the Self—the center of our being, the Divine within us, and the central archetype of our being.

The Self is also seeking us at the same time, orchestrating our lives and acting as an inner teacher if we can learn to participate in life on the symbolic level. The Self puts us on the road to our spiritual quest—which is to become fully human—puts us on the road to discovering "the truth of our own reality," and puts us on the road to discovering the real meaning of love. If we seek greater consciousness through confronting our experiences and ourselves, the Self will guide us. And it will transform us, which means that it will transform our egos by a process of life, death, and renewal, or what the great German poet Goethe called, "the eternal process of creation, destruction and re-creation."

### Transformation: Goethe
### creation → destruction → re-creation

From this perspective, it becomes apparent that we have two important forces in our lives. First is the Self, which is a presence, a force in our lives that is dynamic, and Jung literally refers to it as God within us or the Divine within us. And, second, the actual way the Self works, which is a force of transformation in our lives...a force which works through creation, destruction, and re-creation. In addition, it is helpful for us to keep in mind that the Self works on and through our egos—who we think we are, who we experience ourselves to be—and in our lives.

---

## Two Important Forces in Our Lives

1. The Self
2. The Way of the Self – Transformation

---

Naturally, our ego wants safety, security, and control, because otherwise life can be terrifying. So, even when we are seeking individuation, we are resistant to the Self and fail to realize that the good life is the enemy of a better one. What this longing for safety means is that we all want peace of mind, good relationships, spiritual growth, and a fulfilling life—but we also want to keep our lifestyles and habits, or slightly improved versions of them, at a minimum expenditure of time and effort. And even if we dedicate time and effort, we want to grow joyfully and successfully. In a symbolic sense, we are afraid of the dark. We are afraid of life and circumstances that we can't control and have no experience in how to adapt to.

It is this intrinsic desire in all of us that caused Jung to define God by saying "To this day God is the name by which I designate all things which cross my willful path violently and recklessly, all things which upset my subjective views, plans and intentions and change the course of my life for better or worse." (Jung quoted in *Ego and Archetype* by Edward Edinger, p. 101)

No wonder Dr. Jung was also fond of quoting from Proverbs, "The beginning of Wisdom is the fear of the Lord." The workings of the Self will always upset the way we want to plan, control and envision our lives and goals. A symbolic life is grounded in the quest for consciousness and is a life of discovery, trust and deepening as the spiritual life, or the second half of life, is meant to be. Goals in general are for the first half of life, when we are building our identities and competencies in relationships and careers. In the second half of life—the discovery half—even what we are meant to do or accomplish, as well as the purpose supporting it, must evolve from the process of discovery—of seeking self-knowledge.

---

## First Half of Life – The Building Half

- Identity
- Competence in relationships
- Competence in career or occupation

## Second Half of Life – The Discovery Half

- Learning and discovering turns inward
- Doing evolves from being and discovering
- Becoming more fully human, results from knowing our depths

---

## Questions to Expand Our Understanding

1. How have these ideas of Jung have affected you?
2. What feelings are coming up in you?
3. Are you surprised in any way?

---

**Other Fears**

Now, I believe that there are other fears as well, that make our fear of transformation or God deeply and even unconsciously intense. They are:

1. The fear of waking up, becoming conscious, and realizing life, our lifestyle, friends and family aren't what we thought they were.
2. The fear of being alone—out of the tribe—old and alone, a bag-lady—I've heard this so many times—or T. S. Eliot's J. Alfred Prufrock

3. The fear of losing our self-image and the self-respect we have so carefully constructed (our persona, success, respect, trustworthiness, etc.).
4. The fear of being confused, overwhelmed, and unable to cope with life—which often means we have embraced the illusion that we have control over our life.
5. The fear of having to cope with or of creating chaos (being out of control).
6. The fear of being shamed and seen as inferior, sick, or broken (despite the reality that all new creation comes from chaos and brokenness). The fear of our demons, desires, shameful or raging aspects, and that our caged Mr. Hyde or Medea will get out of control.
7. The fear that our sexuality can become overpowering.

---

### Questions to Expand Our Understanding

1. Now, do you have any thoughts or feelings to journal about this?

---

We know from what we have studied so far that Jung's visionary intellect and profound spirituality have helped many of us heal by learning that our wounds actually open the door to a larger reality—a reality which has been blocked by our one-sided perspective, the point of view we were indoctrinated into.

Dr. Jung has taught us that real suffering, the suffering we use our inauthentic or neurotic pain to defend against, will lead us to wisdom and depth of character. In addition, he teaches us that we unconsciously pathologize because we no longer know how to mythologize. This means that we slide into depression, anxiety, despair, and regression because we have lost the thread of transformation spun by our inner teacher. Individuation is the road home where we discover the unconscious is also the home of the Muses and the abode of angels. Seeking self-knowledge requires commitment and it is hard, but in the long run, suffering and discouragement can become a doorway to joy, beauty, and life's glory.

So, in our world of busyness and an approach to life that suffocates the soul, Jung brings an alternative that is calling us to listen to the voice within, which as the wise old Jungian woman, Helen Luke, tells us, is a voice that is also calling us to live with a noble spirit and the courage of a lion.

## Questions to Expand Our Understanding

1. Now, let me pause for a minute and ask you again what kind of thoughts and feelings are coming to mind for you?

## Phoenix, Moth, and Fire

Now, let us look at images of the Phoenix and the Moth—two archetypal images. The one thing they have in common is "Fire"— the consuming flame. To understand what fire means in transformation, we must think about what it has meant in the human story. We have a hard time imagining what fire must have meant to primitive people. It was their only light in the dark…It provided safety against the dangers of the night…It provided the warmth of life against the cold. To keep the fire or maintain the living coals when a tribe moved was often a sacred and honored job.

Fire is our greatest image of living awareness, the light of consciousness in the Human. This was the gift to Humanity, stolen from the gods, for which both Mantis and Prometheus had to suffer.

In myths and tales, fire represents emotions and passions which can either burn or spread light. The fire of passion compels one to sacrifice an attitude that is too cerebral, and also enables one to realize the spirit. In alchemy, fire indicates one's participation in the work and is equated with the passion one gives to the different stages of growth.

Fire is also transformation and purification. It burns away the impurities. "He has been tested by fire." The fire of emotions in men and women [and often in ourselves] sometimes scares us to death. But without the fire of emotions, no development takes place, and no higher consciousness can be reached. For this reason God says,

"But, because you are lukewarm, neither hot nor cold, I will spit you out of my mouth." (Rev. 3:16) If someone is dispassionate about life and does not suffer—if one has neither the fire of despair nor hatred nor conflict nor love nor annoyance nor anything of that kind, then that person has little growth and little life.

So, fire, whether it represents the negative conflict, hatred, jealousy, or any other effect, speeds up the transformation process and is a type of "judge" that clarifies things. People who have fire may run into trouble and may suffer despair from the destructive aspects of emotional outbursts, but at the same time, if that fire is extinguished, all is lost. We can have too much or too little fire, but make no mistake about it: fire is life itself.

---

### Questions to Expand Our Understanding

1. Isn't it frightening to think of the many ways we are taught to smother our fire?
2. Can you name a few?

---

### The Moth

Now, let me say a few more words about the moth, the "butterfly of the night" that seeks the flame until it is consumed. The shallow interpretation of this image is that it is the soul seeking the Divine until it is consumed by mystical love. But this interpretation is inaccurate if we are one of the *twice born*, and I will explain that term in a few minutes. We do not need to be devoured by Divine love, nor do we need for the Divine, in whatever form you wish to call it, to relate to us as if it is a "good enough" mother showering its baby with unconditional love. Seeing the Divine in this way reduces us to helpless infants that, in fact, the Divine has no real or meaningful need for.

There is a false mystical path, which I refer to as narcissistic mysticism. It is a path where some people think we can lose ourselves in the Divine love and transcend this life. That is a false path. Until we are *twice born*, however, we will tend to seek a Divine figure or spiritual path that wraps us in security and love, or detachment and peace.

The true mystical path, like individuation, calls us to transform through self-knowledge, to follow the path of self-knowledge until it leads to the Divine, or in psychological terms, the Self. The true mystical path leads us to become *twice born*—to know that the Divine's path of creation is transformation—and to then become a co-creator of the world with the Divine.

The moth is relentlessly attracted to the flame as we should be attracted to life. This attraction should never let up until we know it is time to relax into death, our final consummation by life. Nikos Kazantzakis, in his great epic poem, *The Odyssey: A Modern Sequel,* has Odysseus tell us to love our fate, build it beyond ourselves, and pursue the adventure and purpose of our lives until nothing is left unused or unlived at the end and we have burned our lives into ashes. This is the passion for life that he and Jung have defined, and they both made it very clear that our love of life should be constant in life's darkness and in its light, so that the abundance of life that we experience will overflow the boundaries of death.

It is very clear to me that Jung's earlier definition of God—that is, God as a force moving across our path, a force challenging us to transformation when it is least expected—is no sentimental God of motherly love or even fatherly love, for that matter. We will soon see that love for the *twice born* is something very different.

---

### Questions to Expand Our Understanding

1. Before I go on to discuss the twice born, has what I have said about the moth and the flame and being consumed by a love of life made sense?

---

### *Twice Born* – Transformation

OK, now let's get to the discussion of the twice born. Jung uses the term *twice born* repeatedly in Volume 5 of the Collected Works, *Symbols of Transformation.* By this he means we are born first from our mothers into our families and cultures. To be twice born means to have accomplished the first half of life's tasks, and then having made the inner journey back into our unconscious—the symbolic mother of our consciousness—in order to be born again: transformed. Then we are born into a new circle of brothers and sisters, our mother has become the archetypal depths of the Self and our family is now humanity. The people who haven't been twice born are not fully matured and are driven in some form by personal neediness. They have a false reaction to the world. They react as a child toward parents: oversensitive, rebellious, combative, and often sulky, while at the same time being fearful, demanding love, understanding, and emotional rewards. Such people behave like their parents did in many cases, or they follow the customs of our social character because they cannot find their own character.

In fact, the Self or the unconscious will attempt to "throw up" a person seeking safety in being unconscious, by living in an illusion of life, especially the illusion of a good life or a too carefully controlled one, based upon fear and their parents' or the culture's definitions. The Self will often do this by putting us in situations that require a new heroic response, such as a depression or an illness.

Please keep in mind here that the true heroic path is to carry the burden of ourselves and to seek the consciousness that can heal and free us. The *heroic complex*, however, is different. It is trying to overcome and control life by power and expansion. In fact, this complex means a person is still caught in the "mother": unconscious dependency needs. Such a person is approaching life in an adolescent manner, often seeming to be acting out if you look at him or her closely.

When we try to overcome life with insight, power, and expansion—which is actually a defense against carrying the real burdens of our life and becoming *twice born*—our efforts never fully work in the long term. That's because the patterns of our needs and anxieties, and the complexes behind them, have not been transformed. Anyone who has been chronically overweight or addicted can testify to this reality.

The *twice born* have gone through all of the metaphorical struggles of passing through a gestation and birth process, a process that frees us from the comforting feelings that call us to regress during times of challenge into the arms of fear, busyness, conventional wisdom, obligations, responsibilities, and the religious values, family values, and so on, that can rescue us from the confrontation with ourselves, our purposes, the meaning of our lives, and personal destiny.

The development of consciousness through self-knowledge leads to separation not only from the real mother, the symbolic mother, and the pull to be unconscious and to sleepwalk through life but also from the father, our whole family circle, and the power of our instincts.

"Fire making," Jung says (C. W. 5, p. 211) "is a pre-eminently conscious act and therefore 'kills' the dark state of union with the mother." Therefore, we have come full circle here, being sure we are fully engaging in life, reflecting on our experiences, putting what we learn into action, and knowing this process creates a life that is fully alive and transforming.

---

## Questions for Reflection

1. Can you hold the tensions between deep values, powerful social obligations, and your responsibility to the Self?

2. Reflect on the statement:
   Who we are doesn't change – What we are does change.

---

### The Phoenix

This discussion now brings us to the symbol of the Phoenix. From the ancient accounts given by Herodotus and Plutarch, the Phoenix is a dramatically beautiful and striking mythological bird that had the power to be reborn from its own ashes. When the time of its death drew near, it built a nest of aromatic twigs in which it burned from the heat of its own body. This process clearly displays the aspects of its symbolism—the cycle of regeneration, resurrection, and an eternal process of transformation. The Phoenix, whose fire comes from its own body, in the aromatic nest that it built, symbolizes the destructive and creative fire that brings transformation to life through us.

This myth reminds me of the dream of Jacob's ladder—which came while he was on a journey—a dream that told him when we are at the top, we must come down, and when we are at the bottom, we must struggle for a new beginning. When we find ourselves in a bleak place, when everything has disintegrated into ashes, we must respond with the creation of fire, becoming conscious of and open to the Self, or the Divine, catching us in the "hidden hands" of support that Jung spoke of in Memories, Dreams, Reflections. As we allow ourselves to be held and our old selves to burn away, something unexpected emerges and brings a fresh surge of meaning and inspiration from within, which will help us begin to climb the ladder again.

So, we have Fire as the archetypal symbol of the intensity of an engaged life; the Moth as a symbol of our seeking a full engagement with life and the Phoenix as the symbol of transformation by conscious participation.

| | | |
|---|---|---|
| **Fire** | → | the intensity of an engaged life |
| **Moth** | → | seeking full engagement in life |
| **Phoenix** | → | being transformed by a conscious participation in the engagement of life |

## Questions to Expand Our Understanding
We have really covered a lot of ground.
1. What kind of thoughts and feelings are you having?

### In Summary
The work we have been talking about here is hard on the surface. It is difficult to hear that to want unconditional love, acceptance, and understanding—which never means that care and tenderness must

be lost—can be seen as a regression to the unconscious as a child. It almost sounds brutal. But, we have to keep in mind that in his book *Ego and Archetype: Individuation and the Religious Function of the Psyche*, the analyst Edward Edinger uses the crucifixion as a metaphor for the transformation of the ego. And yet, Jung says that we can depend upon the hidden hands of the Self to support us when everything else has failed us. This seems like a contradiction. However, Jung also goes on to say in C.W. 11, *Answer to Job*, that: "It is quite right, therefore, that fear of God should be considered the beginning of all wisdom. On the other hand, the much-vaunted goodness, love, and justice of God should not be regarded as mere propitiation [a pleasing statement], but should be recognized as a genuine experience, for God is a *coincidentia oppositorum*. Both are justified, the fear of God as well as the love of God."

Therefore, we can depend upon the love of God or the Self, not to rescue us or give us what we want, but to move us challengingly and creatively toward wholeness. And, if our love of life is passionate, we can depend upon our "depths" for support, especially when our ego is overwhelmed. But, this doesn't mean we should regress into childhood dependency and the unconscious acceptance of life.

Until we have confronted our shadow, pursued the inner journey, and become *twice born*, our efforts at love will reflect needy psychological pursuits, idealistic fantasies, or sentimental hopes. But, if we are seeking self-knowledge, we will discover that the Self is working, even through these events, as an inner teacher seeking to heal and bring wholeness to us.

I would like to close with my favorite page in Jung's writing, the final page in the chapter titled, "Late Thoughts" in *Memories, Dreams, Reflections*. Jung says:

> For we are in the deepest sense the victims and the instruments of cosmogonic "love." I put the word in quotation marks to indicate that I do not use it in its connotations of desiring, preferring, favoring, wishing, and similar feelings, but as something superior to the

individual, a unified and undivided whole. Being a part, man cannot grasp the whole. He is at its mercy. He may assent to it, or rebel against it; but he is always caught up by it and enclosed within it. He is dependent upon it and is sustained by it. Love is his light and his darkness, whose end he cannot see. "Love ceases not"—whether he speaks with the "tongues of angels," or with scientific exactitude traces the life of the cell down to its uttermost source. Man can try to name love, showering upon it all the names at his command, and still he will involve himself in endless self-deceptions. If he possesses a grain of wisdom, he will lay down his arms and name the unknown by the more unknown, *ignotum per ignotius*— that is, by the name of God. That is a confession of his subjection, his imperfection, and his dependence; but at the same time a testimony to his freedom to choose between truth and error.

# PART TWO

*"The fear of complexes is a rooted prejudice, for the superstitious fear of anything unfavorable has remained untouched by our vaunted enlightenment. This fear provokes violent resistance whenever complexes are examined, and considerable determination is needed to overcome it."*

— C. G. JUNG, C. W. VOL. 8, PAR. 211

*"The fundamental task of the complex is to serve as a vehicle and vessel of transformation, whereby the archetypal essence is brought into living reality. The complex brings archetypal core and personal experience to bear on each other, uniting them in the flow of psychic life."*

— E. SHALIT, *THE COMPLEX*, P. 68

*"In Jung's view, suffering in human life is never an illness as such; rather, it presents the opposite pole to happiness, and the one is unthinkable without the other. A complex becomes pathogenic only when it is repressed, suppressed, or denied in that we think that we don't have it. A complex turns into a negative and disruptive element in the psyche only due to the ego-complex's insufficient capacity to face it."*

— HANS DIECKMANN, *COMPLEXES*, P. 3

*"As events in wartime have clearly shown, our mentality is distinguished by the shameless naiveté with which we judge our enemy, and in the judgment we pronounce upon him we unwittingly reveal our own defects: we simply accuse our enemy of our own unadmitted faults."*

— C. G. JUNG, C. W. VOL. 8, PAR. 516

# Chapter 3 : Lecture

# A LIFETIME OF PROMISE:
## A Jungian Guide to Discovering the Transformative Power in Complexes

## The Character of Complexes

Whenever we begin to study complexes, a lot of emotion and history can become stirred up in us. So, I am going to ask you to fasten your seat belts and to remember Captain Kirk's words whenever a Klingon Battlecruiser began to fire on the Starship *Enterprise*: "Full power to the shields, Mr. Scott." So, let us begin…

In the same way that atoms and molecules are the invisible components of physical objects, complexes are the building blocks of our psychic structure, and the source of our emotional energy. When complexes are realized and integrated, they become the architecture of a fulfilled life.

Like the stone the builder rejected, our most devilish and frustrating complexes hold the most promise for expanding our personalities and our lives. These are the kind of complexes we will focus on in this lecture and then in the seminar. Each one of these complexes can be very destructive and drain our energy as we defend against them like a chronic illness. They disrupt our relationship with ourselves, destroy our self-esteem, and erode the nature of our relationships.

But each of these complexes also holds an inspiring challenge and the promise of transformation—the potential of a greater experience of life. Learning how to discover this challenge and unleash the transformative power in a complex renews our energy, reconnects us to its source, and enables this transformed complex to become the cornerstone in the new design of a more creative life.

Now I would like to tell you a story of one of my encounters with a complex and how the story worked out. As I am talking, keep in mind that true humility comes from confronting our shadows—those things we have repressed that are threatening to our identity, our sense of safety, and our self-respect—and that our shadow is made up of complexes.

With that in mind, I've titled my story, "Complexes are Humbling." The story begins when Brian, a man in his mid-forties came in for his analytic session. Brian had been working with me for several years and his individuation process had led him into a sense of vocation, a loving family life, and financial success. As Brian sat down, he mentioned that he and his wife had lunch over the weekend with several friends who were also, or had been, in analysis with me. I wasn't too surprised because after all I do live in a small town.

Brian said that at one point the conversation had turned to Jung, the journey of individuation, and then to me. "Wade said," Brian continued, "'Bud has a unique way of putting his arm around your shoulder and kicking your rear end at the same time.'"

Then with a smile, Brian said, "And I added, 'Putting his hand in your pocket at the same time.'" I was stunned at this comment. Then I could feel my anger beginning to surge. But, you see, that I also know from the intensity of my reaction that a complex had been touched—or constellated in Jungian terms—which means the intense concentration of emotions in the complex had been aroused. It's like someone has bumped an infected wound very hard.

Realizing a complex had been hit, I was able to compartmentalize it and keep my professional persona intact. That night, in my journal, I was able to work with this experience in the way I will outline for you in a few minutes, and develop further in the seminar. That night was also the beginning of this lecture.

Even in the moment, I knew if I had reacted angrily or confronted Brian's statement as being passive-aggressive, untrue, or even a projection or part of the transference, I would have aborted the potential growth in this situation for both of us.

Now don't misunderstand me. I don't mean that legitimate anger should be avoided. I mean that we need to know ourselves well enough to tell if our intense feelings are legitimate or are coming from a complex. Journaling that evening I began to uncover the potentials for growth. Here is a synopsis of that part of my inner work:

1. For years I secretly resented paying for analysis—until I went to Zurich and realized how priceless this experience of self-discovery really is and how it was revolutionizing my life. Why did I resent paying for something priceless? The answers are:

    a. Pride—I didn't want to admit I was so wounded and screwed up that I couldn't achieve this kind of life on my own. (Nor can most people.)

    b. I was cheap. I had a huge cheap/scarcity complex that I kept hidden deep in my shadow while taking big risks in business and in my life, especially financial risks.

2. This complex hurt me tangibly—cheap clothes, putting off doctor and dentist visits, and having compensatory spending sprees at times—expensive vacations, etc.

3. It hurt my wife—I unconsciously gave off the feeling that she didn't contribute enough—this hampered our efforts at intimacy, distanced us, and devalued her.

4. It hurt my children as well. I devalued them and their wants and needs, in small ways, often with passive aggressive remarks—which really means cruel remarks.

    As you can see, if you begin to really work on your complexes you can't avoid humility. It becomes real. And finally,

5. I didn't want to give my analyst the appreciation he or she deserved or to think that "I" might have a transference.

Reflecting on these issues and complexes led me back to some older and deeper ones that I have worked with for years, such as "I am alone," "I have to do it all myself," and "I can trust and rely on only myself." From the progression in my work you can see that complexes are interlinked. They do not stand alone. Each one has a family tree, so to speak.

At this point I decided that it was time to talk with Brian about his statement and my reaction. In practice, I share these kinds of things very carefully, after giving them a lot of thought. In this case, I felt that Brian had the ego strength to hear me and that he shared some of the same complexes.

As we sat down in his next session, I reminded him of our previous conversation and he actually responded that, "I thought about what I said later and realized it wasn't very nice." I went on to share how I worked with my complex and essentially what I have just told you. While I was going over my list of complexes, Brian became very quiet. When I finished there were several moments of silence. Slowly he said, "I can identify with everything you said. We've got some work to do." Brian was right. We had some work to do. And, it's helpful if we know a few things before we begin.

## What is a Complex?

I think most of us would like to know more about what a complex is, what it does, how we spot it, and then what are the steps we need to take to integrate it into our personality. And this is how I'm going to proceed, beginning with the question—what is a complex. Our complexes come from our deepest human experiences. They begin with how we experience our mother and father. They are formed by the emotional encounters that shape us, usually or most notably the negative and traumatic ones, because growing up is always difficult and a struggle even in the best of circumstances.

If we simply look at the psychoanalyst Erik Erickson's developmental phases, we see that each one of them is marked by a crisis. The names he has given these crises tell us of their intense and dramatic nature—for example, basic trust versus basic mistrust; autonomy versus shame and doubt; initiative versus guilt; industry versus inferiority; identity versus identity confusion; and intimacy versus isolation. Every step in growing up presents a major challenge and the potential of a trauma that can cause a whole village of complexes to develop. Many of these complexes form to protect our vulnerable child-self from shame, guilt, trauma, fear, or some other overwhelming emotion. Complexes can also result from injunctions like "Don't be stupid. Do it yourself. Please your parents. Please your teachers." And this doesn't even get us into the big stuff like violence, abuse, illness, loss of a parent, or having disturbed parents.

Complexes that will affect our lives generally have to do with relationships. The way others respond to us, as we grow up, shapes our view of ourselves and the world. Once we awaken to a complex, we face a task—a journey—yet this journey isn't back to normal, for in Jungian terms there is also a promise. The promise of the journey is to have an enlarged life of increased empowerment and authenticity; and if this complex is a central or dominant one—a destiny. If you read my first book, now re-titled *The Resurrection of the Unicorn: Masculinity in the 21ˢᵗ Century*, you can see behind the pages, my personal story of working through my mother complex and then into the full meaning of being a man.

The promise in a complex comes from its archetypal foundation. Archetypes are the psychological blueprints in our makeup for how our experiences and emotions can be channeled. Let me read to you what Jung says about the archetypes in his essay, "The Significance of the Father in the Destiny of the Individual." (C.W. 4)

> Man "possesses" many things which he has never acquired but has inherited from his ancestors. He is not born a *tabula rasa*, he is merely born unconscious. But he brings with him systems that are organized and ready to function in a specifically human way, and these he owes to millions of years of human development. Just as the migratory and

nest-building instincts of birds were never learnt or acquired individually, man brings with him at birth the ground-plan of his nature, and not only of his individual nature but of his collective nature. These inherited systems correspond to the human situations that have existed since primeval times: youth and old age, birth and death, sons and daughters, fathers and mothers, mating, and so on. Only the individual consciousness experiences these things for the first time, but not the bodily system and the unconscious…

I have called this congenital and pre-existent instinctual model, or pattern of behaviour, the archetype.

Archetypes are like hidden magnets in our psyche that attract and pattern our experiences and emotions. For example, if my father is bombastic, aggressive and shames me for being timid and quiet, I will find my emotions defensively patterned by fear into withdrawal, and the reluctance to express myself. On a deeper level, I will have anger and resentment for his failure to value and understand me. I will have developed a negative father complex. That complex will flood me with fear, confusion, anger and resentment whenever I encounter a bombastic or aggressive authority figure.

But every archetypal image has two poles. The negative father has its opposite, the positive father. The unrealized potential of the opposite pole offers the possibility for growth and transformation. The complex provides the link between the archetypal potential and our ego (our sense of who we are). In other words, when we do the work of integrating a complex, who we think we are is radically transformed. Our ego, our personality has found new strength and emotional balance. We will begin looking at how to integrate a complex in Part B of the lecture.

In summary, a complex is a storehouse for the intense personal emotions we experienced around an event or series of events that are connected to a typical pattern of development or activity in our personality. The complex will cause us to act in ways that protect us from these emotions. Its potential for growth lies in its call to us to heal our past, release the energy the complex is costing us and experience the new growth that is now possible.

## What Does a Complex Do?

Next let us ask ourselves: What does a complex do? Actually, we all have some familiarity with complexes and what they do. Haven't we heard of and even used terms like an *inferiority complex*, a *superiority complex*, and haven't we had a relative who tried to manipulate us with their victim complex? Power complexes are notable in bosses, colleagues, and organizations. We've heard of messianic complexes, mother complexes, father complexes, and so on, until the word has become fairly common. What this familiarity means is that a complex can have enough power to take over someone's personality or our own, to the point that it becomes apparent to everyone except the person who has it. And, when it has done this to us, it determines our worldview, our emotional responses, and how we feel about ourselves.

Let's look at a couple of typical examples. A man with a negative mother complex will tend to feel criticized whenever women do anything other than praise him. He, of course, has this inner witch that is criticizing him constantly or making him think he is living the wrong life. This complex keeps his masculinity in a weak position and hinders his ability to initiate his life relationships and healthy confrontations. He fears being devoured by the feminine and will often project this complex onto women and then fail to see them as who they really are, and fail to protect his boundaries appropriately.

The woman with a negative mother complex will feel that she is an awful person in a rejecting world. She may seek out soft or wounded males who appear to have "good mothering qualities" such as appearing nurturing, accepting, and sensitive. An inner voice of fear, anxiety, and distrust as well as the feeling she has no right to exist will remind her constantly of how hard she needs to strive to earn love; and even then it is unlikely to come or to be trustworthy. And, she will try to control what happens around her.

These two examples are greatly oversimplified, but are common enough that we can understand them. The man's inner witch and the woman's inner tyrant are complexes that will drain their energy, self-confidence, and relations like a chronic disease.

When one of these complexes is activated, we become very defensive. The complex crowds everything else into the background. It inhibits all other ideas, and shapes everything going on to fit its perspective. It pushes any thoughts or feelings that run counter to it into the unconscious.

In our ordinary experience, the feeling of being taken over by a complex is often referred to as "I was beside myself" or "I don't know what got into me." But, if the complex is strong enough, we will be absolutely convinced of the rightness of our position and will find endless arguments to support it.

Frequently these arguments may simply be within ourselves. If, because of the early wounds in our formative years, we over-identify with the need for safety, which means control and often power, and have a self-concept based on achievement, we may feel like we can't slow down, we can't stop driving ourselves. Actually, these are complexes that our society supports. But they create the kind of stress that can destroy our health, as can any complex that demands perfectionism. In many cases our choices are either to become the victim of our complexes or to wake up to them and learn how to integrate them.

In summary, a negative complex can momentarily put our life off track and embarrass us, or become an increasing source of neurosis, or if it is strong enough and repressed forcefully enough, it can impair or even destroy our health.

We have covered a lot of ground in a few minutes. I began with the story of my experience of a complex. Then I went on to answer the questions, "What is a complex? And what does a complex do?"

And I will talk about how we spot these complexes in the next section. The only thing I would like to add at this point is the worst shape we can be in, is to think we don't have any complexes, or only a few. This kind of unconscious naiveté or denial simply means that our complexes have us, and we have lost touch with our potentials for growth and transformation.

---

**Questions to Expand Our Understanding**

1. As I have talked about my experience of a complex, what kind of thoughts, memories, and questions came to mind for you?

2. What are some of your questions about the emotions complexes arouse in our lives?

3. What kinds of thoughts and feelings came up in my discussion of complexes draining our energy like a chronic illness?

4. What do you think about my statement that if we think we don't have any complexes then they have us?

---

## The Heroic Journey Out of Cultural Complexes and Into Self-Acceptance

### How do we spot these complexes?

I promised in the last section to discuss how we can identify these complexes. I have already said and most of you already know that we—and that means our egos—are not in complete charge of our lives. There are a number of moods that can sweep over us—things we have been conditioned into and forces that drive us. Whether we sneak food, have too many glasses of wine every night, snap at our partners or co-workers or scream at our kids, we find ourselves doing things we wouldn't choose to do. Complicated bundles of feelings lurk in the complexes we work so hard to overcome or repress. When they are touched, they leap out at our ego like a troll who has hidden under a bridge, and thwart our best intentions and activities.

Complexes have symptoms and we can learn to look out for these symptoms. Major complex symptoms are often shown in our moods or emotional overreactions. I knew at once that my anger at Brian's remark was an overreaction to the reality of the situation. An excess of hurt, fear, anger, or even a bad or sulky mood is the mark of a complex. So is the absence of hurt, fear, or anger, when such feelings should be appropriate. A combination of being excessively angry and judgmental is the sure sign of a complex.

Chronic emotional problems such as anxiety, depression, jealousy, envy, and addictions are usually signs that we are repressing a serious complex. Physical problems, weight problems, and other such things are the signs we have repressed a complex with such force that the complex has gone into our bodies.

One of our favorite defenses is to project our complex onto someone else. As long as we keep our consciousness limited, we can more easily confuse our inner and outer worlds. It is much easier, for example, for a man to project his inner witch onto his partner or female boss than to confront her as part of himself; or for a woman to project her inner tyrant onto the culture, her partner, or boss. The more unconscious we are, the more we use our own inner material to "create" the characters of the people around us. Of course, projection can become a gold mine for developing self-knowledge, though such mining is painful and humbling.

Journaling, reflecting on our feelings and relationships throughout the day and the moods they left us in, helps us discover complexes. So do dreams. The figures that threaten us, pursue us, ignore us, or even the ones that just show up can be picturing a complex that can expand our personhood. A few sessions after I had talked with Brian and he had tackled a couple of new complexes he said, "Damn, this is really hard work. I can see why Scott Peck opened his book, *The Road Less Traveled*, with the statement, 'Life is difficult,' and then said, 'Many are called, few are chosen, and they are dragged through the door kicking and screaming.'"

Brian is right. Real change doesn't take a little bit of time; it takes a *lot* of time. And, it doesn't take a little bit of work, it takes a *lot* of work. But, Scott Peck had read enough of Jung to realize the promise in our difficulties, and that the second half of life is a special time. It is a time of great opportunity, emotionally, spiritually, and collectively—a time for love to grow beyond our needy wounds and sentimental ideals—beyond our complexes—and to flourish.

There are few journeys in our life that fit Joseph Campbell's description of the hero's or heroine's journey more accurately than confronting and integrating our complexes. Whether a complex is big or small, confronting it calls for a complete reorientation of our consciousness. This means that we must be willing to give up our present system of ideals, virtues, goals, and formerly successful ways of dealing with our problems, instead of working to make this old system stronger.

For Brian, this also meant that he had to give up the secret hope that had fueled his initial desire to begin his inner work. This was the hope of leading a beautiful, self-actualized life that had previously seemed to be constantly eluding him. Life, it seemed, had been continually throwing roadblocks in his way. In fact, Brian, like many of us, myself included, had wanted to live an "ego-ideal" that compensated for his earlier woundings, secret feelings of inferiority, and longings.

I'll share with you how one of my own complexes became clear to me. For years, maybe decades, I had fantasized about having a Porsche. Then one day I thought I might finally be able to buy one. On the showroom floor was a sleek black Targa, my dream car. I opened the door, smelled the rich leather, and slipped into the driver's seat. Damn! My fantasies crashed to the ground. It was small and cramped and I was eye level with the top of the windshield. When I was forced by fate to think about the symbolic meaning of the Porsche, I realized that for years a negative father complex had caused me to remain hidden within myself, carefully calculating how much of me it was safe to let the world see. The Porsche was a compensatory fantasy from the unconscious that showed an inner desire to move around in the world with power and agility, and to be noticed.

My Self, like Brian's Self, which we both had been out of touch with, had a bigger story in mind for us. But, this story included a series of night-sea journeys into several complexes. In an interesting turn of events, once Brian had worked through some of the complexes that were causing him to long for a beautiful self-actualized life, he discovered his profession was really his vocation.

With that realization, he was able to set aside his complaints about having to work so hard, which like most of us he had blamed on other people and having to make so much money. Then he was able to find pleasure in the pursuit of creativity and excellence in his vocation. Instead of being a burden that drove him, his work became a fulfillment.

It is our complexes that carry our wounds and our wounds are our calls to transformation. In a way, our complexes are our wounds as well, and if we defend against them too forcefully, they turn against us and cripple us. There was a time in my early adulthood when I made it a point to appear capable and competent and to avoid anything that might appear like self-pity. Then I had a dream that I remember today, over forty years later, like it came yesterday.

In the dream, I was eight years old. I was standing next to a bicycle my father had repaired and given to me for Christmas. In actuality, I had been ashamed that we couldn't afford a new one. I was on the campus of the private school my grandfather had founded. I couldn't ride the bike or even push it because I had a cast on my leg that went from the top of my thigh down to my foot.

As long as my ego's coping skills were intact, my childhood vulnerability had remained repressed. But, once transformation began my unconscious was reminding me that a healing journey was needed to secure the foundation for later growth.

This is a hero's journey because it takes me into the dark night on a sea of emotions where my most treasured competencies can't be used because they were part of how I mastered the outer world, and now I had to face the inner one. That's where Campbell tells us the real hero's or heroine's journey must be, even though it will bring us back into the outer world, in a renewed form.

In a certain sense, Brian and I—for as you heard I too am on this journey—have to face our fear of death. For the fear of death is about the fear of change, or the fear of growing up, or the fear of becoming independent of the claims of the material world, or a fear of questioning the responsibilities and obligations we have used to define ourselves.

When I had my dream, I was facing a major life decision about whether to leave the corporate world and start my own business, as something inside of me was compelling me to do. My fantasies of outer success were met by their image of vulnerability and the need for healing from my unconscious. Campbell tells us that our calls often begin with something ugly, just like in a fairy tale—a frog, a wizened old woman, a dragon, a dwarf, or a robber. Our wounds, mistakes, and symptoms are pictured this way, in story form. Our complexes cause ripples on the surface of our lives, produced by the unsuspected springs of an archetype that maybe as deep as the soul itself.

Giving up our complexes is often difficult because as long as we have them, we can repress other things—like facing ourselves and owning our potentials—and find excuses for not wishing to change. Our complexes become a prop, and as long as we can fight them, we can, in Campbell's words, refuse the call and maintain the status quo, which will, in his words, eventually create a waste-land in our lives where our heart should be flourishing.

There is a second way to refuse the call that I actually learned in my early training in humanistic and Gestalt psychology. That was to think I had a breakthrough, to feel the release of tension, and to then think, "I'm back in control, I understand the blockage or problem. Now everything is going to work out, and I'm going to feel good." A breakthrough insight is not the end; it is the beginning because, Jung reminds us, we then have a moral duty to live it, and that is a journey.

We can compound this mistake when we name our complexes in overly simplistic ways such as, "that's my money complex," "that's my negative father speaking," "that's my mother complex" and so on. Naming a complex can be important but it can also be a defense. We must not fall into the typical shadow defense of our culture's scientific complex which is to think that to name something means we have some control over it. I've heard many,

many people say something like, "that's my money complex—but, I'm doing better at it," or "that's my critical mother—but I'm doing better than I used to." This approach is missing the point of healing and transformation. It is simply causing a new inner battle on a different level. It continues to split us against ourselves, rather than helping us find wholeness and solidity.

This error reflects a cultural complex which is that we are taught to live our lives according to the ways of Mars, the god of war and not the ways of Eros, the god of love and relationships. Our society teaches us that war is the way. We declare war on poverty, drugs, cancer, our weight, in fact on whatever symptoms are giving us the most trouble. We declare war on ourselves in this process. And, as far as I can see in my lifetime we rarely, if ever, win these wars.

Why don't we ever win some of these wars, we might wonder? Well, let me suggest an answer on the personal level, because as you know, Jung thought that in today's world that's where change must start. Most of the complexes that really trouble us come from problems in Eros, those related to love and relationships. They are wounds of the lack of love, the lack of understanding and personal concern, the lack of affirmation in childhood, and these events founded our complexes. Even wounds of fate, like my mother's death when I was a child, which was a trauma, brought a wound of Eros because one of its major sources was lost, I was abandoned.

Abuse is a betrayal of Eros. There are, of course, many more than I have named. The point I want to make is that you cannot heal wounds to Eros with the techniques of Mars: aggression, suppression and control. Yet that is what we try to do. We want to overcome, defeat our complexes.

The analyst Erel Shalit in his book, *Enemy, Cripple and Beggar: Shadows in the Hero's Path* tells us that to engage in Eros is to "… recognize and accept, contain and relate to the inferior and suffering side of ourselves. Likewise the capacity to experience internal pain is crucial to our ability to relate, inwardly as well as to others." When Jung was corresponding with Bill Wilson, a cofounder of Alcoholics Anonymous, he said that "*Spiritus contra Spiritus*" was needed for healing. For healing and transforming our complexes I believe we need "*Eros contra Eros.*"

Jolande Jacobi was one of the first Jungian analysts to write a book on complexes. In *Complex/Archetype/Symbol*, she says that we—that is, our egos—have four different approaches to dealing with a complex: The first one is to remain totally unconscious of its existence; the second one is to identify with it—this means that when it takes over we have no choice but to identify with it—it becomes the "I"; the third one is projection, which I have discussed already; and, fourth, is confrontation.

In my way of thinking, confrontation means realizing that we have a complex and that we have to wake up and begin the journey of transforming it. And that journey means going from confrontation to Eros, working in partnership with ourselves instead of being split against ourselves.

As I was working with Margaret, a woman whose story I tell in my book *Sacred Selfishness*, she came upon a troubling complex and didn't want to continue pursuing it. Then, on her next visit she came in and told me she had a dream the night after we had talked. In the dream, she was lying asleep under the water in a shallow pond. The night was bright with moonlight and her cat was sleeping beside her. "Damn" she said, "I'm going to lie there and drown and let my cat drown with me, in water that would hardly come up to my knees. I've got to wake up and get moving or we are going to die." Once we have awakened, we are ready for the journey.

### How do we start the journey?
Before beginning I want to remind you what Joseph Campbell says about it, because I love this saying and it has sustained me for decades. Campbell says:

> …we have not even to risk the adventure alone; for the Heroes of all time have gone before us; the labyrinth is thoroughly known; we have only to follow the thread of the hero-path. And where we had thought to find an

abomination, we shall find a god; where we had thought
to slay another, we shall slay ourselves; where we had
thought to travel outward, we shall come to the center
of our own existence; where we had thought to be alone,
we shall be with all the world.

We are called to confront our complexes by our circumstances,
frustration, and suffering, and by our desire for a more fulfilling
and complete life. It is very helpful if we know that people have
traveled the path before us, that we don't have to plunge blindly
into the unknown. And even though our path must be unique, we
are guided by a chart but not a rigidified doctrine.

We have some legitimate questions as we begin. What will we
encounter? How do we strengthen ourselves for the struggle and
the pain? What will the pain be like? What are our alternatives? Is
there a chart for the territory? What is the reward? Each complex
we integrate releases new energy, broadens and strengthens our personality, adds to our wholeness, and affects the world in the new
way we relate to everyone around us. And we have refined, through
new inner clarity, our ability to see reality in a more accurate way.

In terms of charting the territory I have put together seven
steps for transforming a complex. I want to briefly mention all
seven of them, and then I will examine them one at a time. They
combine eros and transformation and lead us to use our aggression
in the service of wholeness rather than against a part of ourselves.

STEP ONE in transforming a complex is to accept it.

STEP TWO is to amplify it.

STEP THREE is to write a history of it.

STEP FOUR is to give it a name and/or create an image that
symbolizes it.

STEP FIVE is to examine how it affects the events in our lives
every day.

STEP SIX is to use active imagination to dialog with it. And,

STEP SEVEN is to have a special section or box in your journal
to remind you of it daily.

The first step, acceptance, is where *Eros contra Eros* is the turning point. Accepting it doesn't mean loving it or embracing it. After all, the princess didn't embrace the frog. She very reluctantly kissed it. And, a kiss is a transformative act in fairy tales.

If we need to cure, fight, defeat, or overcome a symptom or some attitude or characteristic, we have made our complex into an enemy and are losing the teleological value of it—the potentials to which the complex can guide us. Of course, this perspective is counter-cultural. It negates our ideas of control, rationality, and curing as well as, to some extent, the notion of alleviating human misery. But if, for example, Margaret makes an enemy of the depression that was coming from her complex, she gives it power. The 43rd hexagram in the *I Ching*, "Breakthrough or Resoluteness" notes, "If evil is branded, it thinks of weapons, and if we do it the favor of fighting against it, blow for blow, we lose in the end, because then we ourselves get entangled in the hatred and passion." Or, in other words, we develop a war within ourselves, against ourselves.

When Margaret takes the Jungian position, she immediately gains a certain amount of distance and separation from her depression. It becomes what we call "Not-I." She has differentiated from it. It can no longer possess her totally whenever it is constellated. This separation opens a number of doors: We can relate to the complex differently. We can seek to understand it from the inside. We can learn how it may want us to change our lives in order for us to increase our wholeness.

Taking the Jungian position doesn't mean that we abandon our capacity for being aggressive. If we abandon Mars, then we have to repress him and that creates a hell of a complex. What we must do is hold our capacity for aggression in abeyance until we can make a conscious choice whether to declare war or not. We may end up needing to struggle with some inner aspects of ourselves. But we want to be sure we are working in a way that is constructive, that stands for, and if possible, facilitates growth and transformation. This approach strengthens us, empowers us, eventually inviting wisdom and compassion and deepening our humanity.

Our goal is to transform how we use our energy. We want our work to end up enlivening us, not draining us like the complex did. Warfare takes a lot of resources and should be chosen very carefully. Jung is emphatic that nothing can be transformed until it is accepted. And, this acceptance of ourselves is absolutely necessary to become whole and to be able to nurture, support, and work in partnership with ourselves.

---

### Questions to Expand Our Understanding

We have covered a lot of ideas. I think it is time for us to stop and have some questions and discussion.

1. Did this material bring up any fantasies, feelings, ideas, or questions for you?

2. To what use can you put some of these ideas?

3. What do you feel about using *Eros contra Eros* in dealing with yourself? Think about what complex stands in your way.

4. What are some of your responses to our societal complexes of getting it right, doing it myself, i.e. individualism, and attacking everything rationally?

---

## Journey Into Depth

The session right after I had gone over the seven steps for transforming a complex with Margaret, she came into my office and sat down briefly. "Boy, are you tricky," she said, "You tricked me good." "What do you mean?" I answered. "Well," she said, "I've been working on these steps all week; it's been hard and challenging, but I've opened up a lot. Then I realized that if I'm spending this much time and energy on my life, I really am valuing myself." "Imagine that," I thought to myself, "and I wasn't even trying to be tricky."

Let's continue to look at **STEP ONE**. When we learn to accept the things within us that we feel are truly repulsive or even dangerous to our well-being or self-image, such as selfishness, arrogance, rage, anger, aggression, lust, self-loathing, grief, inauthenticness—things that might make others (especially those close to us) dislike us or disapprove of us or things that we fear may make us despise ourselves—we both open and strengthen our personality.

Acceptance doesn't mean we act on these impulses. We own the ability to experience them, and act on them if we consciously choose to. This opening gives us the strength of personality to then experience the other side of these characteristics, such as love and compassion, in a truly genuine fashion. It will also help us genuinely love and have compassion with ourselves.

Usually when I'm in the throes of working with a complex, I find myself awake in the middle of the night, furious or occasionally in despair—more often furious—and unable to sleep, and the first thing I usually do is project the whole conflict onto my wife and think of a number of great reasons for being angry at her, hurt with her, feeling slighted by her—and all having nothing whatsoever to do with her. At least I've learned that much. Next, I used to go on to my analyst and think of all the ways he or she misunderstood me, didn't see I was right, didn't value my pain sufficiently, and was betraying me. Now I have the capacity to go on a long way with this line of thinking, or rather projecting—sometimes to relatives, friends, or long-dead parents, uncles, and aunts. And while the seeds of some of my imaginings may not be wrong, the way I am pursuing these thoughts is.

That is where **STEP TWO**, amplifying what's going on within me, becomes important. What I mean by amplify is to write down everything that comes to mind about this complex, including all the irrational feelings, with no censorship. This step is akin to what Julia Cameron calls "Morning Pages" in *The Artist's Way*, except that I do it whenever a complex is seizing me or I am working on one. I write down everything I'm feeling about my wife, analyst, or whomever, in just the way it comes. This cleans the sludge out of my psyche, distances me from the feelings, because they are out of my mind and concretely expressed on paper. This procedure allows me to get a more objective perspective on what I'm feeling and better insight into where it's coming from.

In writing about her compulsive eating, at one point Margaret wrote, "This sneaky complex allows me to secretly nourish myself no matter what. It comes quickly and is very intense. It puts my needs first. If it tastes good, eat it. If you're hungry, eat. If you're mad, eat. If you're lonely, eat. If you are sad, eat. If you are frustrated, eat. Nobody has to see you. If you want it, have it...'Oh, Oh'."

There are two important points in this step of amplification. First, no censorship. And, second, don't share any of this with anyone except your analyst. No fair dumping this on a friend or partner. That is really just trying to pass the feelings of your complex on to them. For real transformation we need to hold and contain the tension in our own process.

**STEP THREE** is to write a history of this complex. Go back as far as you can remember with it. Is it a family complex, a complex in the culture you grew up in? Did it come to you through one of your parents? Is it truly yours—that is, based on your wounding— or is it one you inherited because someone passed it on instead of working it out? What were the early emotions around the early wound? What kind of situations have activated these emotions over time and strengthened the complex? These questions are examples and the best ones are the ones you think of. You don't have to write a book, even though I actually found myself doing that. Writing a real history usually helps us have compassion for ourselves and to realize these complexes may have once served to help or protect us. Most people do about one to ten pages.

Margaret said that she found this part exciting because she could begin to see where the complex gave her a pay-off. She could see where she secretly got the best of people and inwardly defied her rigid mother and fundamentalist father. Even those of us who function in life with strong persecution or victim complexes know, at some level, we enjoy the power our misery gives us.

**STEP FOUR** is to give the complex a name and to try to give it an image. Winston Churchill called his depression his "black dog." Giving it a name and an image helps us differentiate from it even more. They confer a separate identity on the complex, which moves it further into the field of our imagination, where it has more distance to travel in order to come back to take us over. The fact of bringing our imagination into play is one of the first steps in transforming a complex from destructive to creative.

For example, when Marsha was struggling with panic attacks, she imaged them as a hurricane. She felt her anticipation of them was like staring at an approaching hurricane: fear, panic, disaster, no control, devastation, impending doom. She named her hurricane complex "Katrina" because it made her feel so devastated and defeated.

Several important things are happening here for Marsha, however. She is accepting her hurricane complex and all of the fear and negativity it brings. She is furthering her relationship with it, by amplifying what it brings to her and by writing a thoughtful history of it—the panic attacks first appeared in adolescence, then left, and returned 20 years later. And by giving the complex distance, and differentiating from it, she is setting the stage for being able to dialog directly with it, which can usually transform such a complex into an inner teacher, though a harsh one at times.

**STEP FIVE** is to examine the activity of the complex in your life through journaling. This means recording how it affects you and the events in your life every day. In general, I believe there are four kinds of journaling. The first is simply keeping a diary. The second is one that repeats over and over again the themes and emotions that our complexes and wounds seem to be keeping us stuck in. It is like we are stuck in the mud and are spinning our wheels; or, in some cases, they become flights of fantasy that compensate the despair we are unable to confront. The third kind is what I've borrowed from Julia Cameron: "Morning Pages." All of these can be helpful in some way and can have their own value. But, the kind of journaling I am referring to in this step is "journaling as inner exploration," (the title of Chapter Five in *Sacred Selfishness*).

In this kind of journaling we are creating and recreating ourselves. We are bringing together both the act of being engaged in life and the act of reflecting on the life we've experienced. In the case of our complexes, we are reflecting on the thoughts and emotions they generate throughout the day and the images they might bring to mind—images like a Porsche, or the one from my dream of holding my bike and having a cast on my leg. In summing up her day's journaling about her panic attacks or hurricane complex, Marsha noted: "This complex is reactionary. It appears in reaction to extreme disharmony or discord in my home. Katrina appears when I am not the source of the problem and feel powerless to confront, or have to act in a way I don't like or admire, in order to confront. Katrina suddenly appears and sweeps everything away."

On their own these kinds of reflections will begin to lead us into transformation. We can start by simply recording the daily events, noting the feelings they evoked in us, and then asking ourselves if they are related to our complex. Then we ask how, and why. Note: Reading Chapter Five of *Sacred Selfishness* might be helpful in this process.

If I were in your place right now, I would be thinking that all this stuff sounds good, but Bud is charting out more than I can ever do. However, cheer up, I'm not saying you have to sit down and do the seven steps every day. Remember Jung says the goal is to be on the journey. If we forget that, and fall into the trap of one or two of our societal complexes, that is, that we have to "achieve" integration and get on with our lives—we will miss the real opportunities that come from working with the material.

I can't use will power to drive this work. I am moved by my love of growth, transformation, and becoming more fully human. Sometimes my psyche can devour hours of this, and sometimes it can only stand a few minutes. I have to respect that. And, I have to be fierce and creative in giving time to myself—and to confronting my achievement complex when my psyche or my anima is saying, "OK Bud, that's enough for now. Digest this and then we will resume."

**STEP SIX** is to dialog with the complex, or one of the major emotions connected to it. Dialoging is part of what we call Active Imagination. Active Imagination gives both form and voice to parts of our personality that normally aren't heard and it sets up lines of communication with them. It means actively expressing ourselves—in writing—in order to help get differentiation, and then "actively" listening to ourselves. And, we must listen in a way that is seeking to understand our complexes and emotions. We are not trying to get them to go away, shut up, or to leave us alone. We don't attack them unless they attack us. And if they do, which is rare in dialoguing, we need to take them quickly to an analyst or therapist. They may attack us with overwhelming emotions, obsessive thoughts and/ot debilitating physical symptoms.

As we learn to talk with our emotions and complexes, which may even be expressed as an illness, we learn to listen to these features in ourselves and understand the parts they play in our lives more clearly. I recommend you read a dialog that I shared in Chapter Six in *Sacred Selfishness*. I must admit that Active Imagination was the hardest thing for me to grasp in Jungian psychology. It took me about five years of effort to really get into it, but the results I now get are priceless. We want to hold it in our awareness in order to see how it's affecting us, how we are affecting it, what it is trying to teach us, and how our deepening relationship with it is changing us and our lives for the better.

And finally, **STEP SEVEN** is to put a special section or box in your journal to remind you of this complex every day. We want to hold it in our awareness, to see how it's affecting us, how we are affecting it, what it is trying to teach us and how our deepening relationship with it is changing us and our lives for the better.

## Seven Steps for Transforming a Complex

Following these Seven Steps softens our ego's stance toward complexes without weakening the ego at all. In fact, it will become stronger as its boundaries soften and relax. In this process, we are combining Eros—the feminine approach to consciousness, reflection, accepting, and relating to—with the masculine approach, Logos—which is separating, differentiating, and bringing into the light.

*Eros* is neither embracing nor welcoming. It is a shift in attitude that begins with acceptance, even if our complex and its emotions look like a deformed dwarf or a hideous witch. Acceptance allows separation to begin and that can be followed by relating to, rather than fighting against. *Eros* needs the help of *Logos* because "relating to" requires separation and differentiation in order to take place. We cannot relate to either a person or a complex that we are fused with or possessed by. This act in itself—the act of separation— helps put us in the position of being able to become more objective and less driven by the obsessive and compulsive nature of the complex.

Bringing the complex, its emotions, and how it affects us into the light of consciousness is also *Logos*. This means that understanding the complex and our feelings brings the energy of the complex into our ego, our conscious personality. When complexes become appropriately assimilated and integrated into our ego, a new openness in our personality develops both toward our inner life and our outer world.

The dynamics of these Seven Steps begins with acceptance which leads to separation and proceeds to "relating to" *Eros* and "learning from" *Logos*. Relating and learning become the path of understanding that leads to knowledge and then to wisdom. Wisdom opens us to a greater experience of life as it informs how we live.

What I have been doing in this lecture is to continue in my vocation of being a spokesperson for individuation, for growth, healing, wholeness and love. In the individuation process we ground ourselves in the part of the feminine that is relational and feeling—that comes from the heart. And, we learn that our inner relationships are the foundation for our outer ones as well as our relationship to life and the Divine.

I intend for my work to be an invitation to accept ourselves more fully. As we find the courage to sacrifice our self-images again and again, we can relate to our complexes and find the promise of an open heart and an enlarged life—a life that is secure in enough self-knowledge to free us from the roles that often reflect needy psychological pursuits, idealistic fantasies, and sentimental hopes.

Individuation requires a choice. It is a choice to choose life in a more abundant sense—to stop sleepwalking through driven, busy days and to find the courage to face ourselves and to work in partnership with our deepest potentials in their struggle to be born.

## Questions to Expand Our Understanding

1. I would like to ask for you to write your reflections, reactions, etc.

2. Did anything surprise you in this section?

3. What did you think and feel about my discussion of "acceptance"?

4. Likewise, do you have any thoughts or reflections on my term *Eros contra Eros*?

## Seven Steps for Transforming A Complex

**Acceptance:** Accepting a complex means fully admitting its existence, power, and emotions. It doesn't mean welcoming it, loving it or embracing it. Acceptance is the first step, and deciding how to relate to it comes later. However, acceptance of and paying conscious attention to anything that has been previously unconscious will begin to change it. Acceptance is the first step in *Eros contra Eros*. It doesn't mean we abandon our capacity to be tough with or aggressive toward a complex. It means we hold these capacities in check until we see a conscious need for them, which actually turns out to be rare.

**Amplify:** Amplifying the complex means to write down everything that I feel or that comes to mind about a complex. "Everything" includes all the irrational, nasty, unpleasant feelings with no censorship. This step is like the "Morning Pages" that Julia Cameron explains in *The Artist's Way*, except I do it whenever the emotion of a complex is seizing me or when I am working on one. I write down everything I'm feeling, which generally is being overly furious, overly judgmental, or overly despairing about how unfairly I'm being treated or misunderstood or not appreciated. I write how I'm feeling about my wife, parents, analyst, or whomever, in just the way it comes. This allows me to accept and experience my emotions and clear the sludge out of my psyche. It also distances me from the feelings because they are out of my mind, and expressed concretely on paper. This procedure helps me get a more objective perspective on what I am experiencing and better insight into where it is coming from.

**History:** Step three is to write a history of the complex. This history begins the process of seeking to understand it. Whenever we meet new friends or lovers, we usually begin the relationship by telling our story and listening to theirs in an effort to know them and be known by them. Go back as far as you can remember with the complex. Is it a family complex, a complex in the culture you grew up in? Did it come to you through one of your parents? Is it truly yours—that is, based on your own wounding—or is it one you inherited because someone passed it on, instead of working it out? What were the early emotions around the early wound? What kinds of situations have activated these emotions over time and strengthened the complex? These questions are examples, and the best ones are the ones you think of. Writing a real history helps us have compassion for ourselves and to realize these complexes may have once served to help or protect us. Most people do about one to ten pages.

**Name it:** Name it and give it an image. Adam, the Biblical ancestor of humankind is given the task of naming all the creatures. In symbolic terms, God has given him the task of distinguishing them consciously. Name is a symbol of becoming conscious of the exact nature of whatever is being named. Go with whatever name comes to mind and don't make this a laborious process. The name that quickly comes to mind is likely to be the one rooted in your unconscious and therefore the most helpful one. Our imagination gives images to or personifies intense emotions and experiences all the time. An image often helps open the door to our interior life. Giving a name and an image (such as Churchill calling his depression his "black dog") requires conscious attention and is the opposite of repression. Giving a complex, or the strong emotion it evokes, a name and an image helps us differentiate from it even more. A name confers a separate identity on the complex, which moves it further into the field of our imagination where it has more distance to travel in order to come back and take us over. The fact of bringing our imagination into play is one of the first steps in transforming a complex from destructive to creative.

**Journaling:** Step five is to examine the activity of the complex in my life through journaling. This means recording how it affects you and the events in your life every day. The kind of journaling I am referring to in this step is "Journaling as Inner Exploration," the title of Chapter Five in *Sacred Selfishness*. In this kind of journaling, we are creating and recreating ourselves. We are bringing together the act of being engaged in life with the act of reflecting on the life we've experienced. In the case of our complexes, we are reflecting on the thoughts, emotions, and images they generate throughout the day. On their own, these reflections will begin to lead us into transformation. We can start by simply recording daily events, noting the feelings they evoked in us, and then asking ourselves if these feelings are related to our complex. Then we ask how and why. Reading Chapter Five of *Sacred Selfishness* might be helpful.

**Dialog:** Step six is to dialog with the complex or one of the major emotions connected to it. Dialoging is part of what we call Active Imagination. Active Imagination gives both form and voice to parts of our personality that normally aren't heard, and it sets up lines of communication with them. It means actively expressing ourselves in writing, in order to help get differentiation, and then "actively" listening to ourselves. And we must listen in a way that is seeking to understand our complexes and emotions. We are not trying to get them to go away, to shut up, or to leave us alone. We don't attack them unless they attack us, and if they do, which is rare, we need to take them quickly to an analyst or therapist. As we learn to talk with our emotions or complexes, which may even be expressed as an illness, we learn to listen to these features in ourselves and understand the parts they play in our lives more clearly. Chapter Six in *Sacred Selfishness*, "Dialoging as Interrelating" reflects my journey of working through and into Active Imagination. It is truly *Eros contra Eros*.

**Staying Aware of the Complex:** Step seven is to put a special section or box in your journal to remind you of this complex every day. We want to hold it in our awareness in order to see how it is affecting us, how we are affecting it, what it is trying to teach us, and how our deepening relationship with it is changing us and our lives for the better. Some people also include a short meditation on the complex to help them stay aware of it.

*Please keep in mind that inner work is not meant to be like running a marathon or achieving a winning position. According to Jung, the goal is to be on the journey. If we forget this and fall into the trap of one or two of our societal complexes—that is, we have to achieve integration and get on with our lives—we will miss the real opportunities and surprises that come from truly working with the material.*

# Chapter 4 : Seminar

## A LIFETIME OF PROMISE:
### A Jungian Guide to Discovering the Transformative Power in Complexes

### Big M and Big F

After the lecture last night, Massimilla said that I had better start this morning's seminar with a joke. I replied, "That's a good idea. You better get me one about fathers and mothers." And, she did. It is about Fred who is 32 years old and still single.

*One day a friend of Fred's asked, "Why aren't you married? Can't you find a woman who will be a good wife?"*

*Fred replied, "Actually, I've found many women I wanted to marry, but when I bring them home to meet my parents, my mother doesn't like them."*

*His friend thinks for a moment and says, "I've got the perfect solution, just find a girl who's just like your mother."*

*A few months later they meet again and his friend says, "Did you find the perfect girl? Did your mother like her?"*

*With a frown on his face, Fred answers, "Yes, I found the perfect girl. She was just like my mother. You were right, my mother liked her very much."*

*The friend said, "Then what's the problem?"*

*Fred replied, "My father doesn't like her."*

With that I want to pick up where I mentioned last night that our mother complex and father complex, big M and big F, are the parents of all of our major complexes. You can't imagine my surprise when I discovered this fact during my analytic training. I was in my late forties. I had been to years of therapy and I thought, I *thought*, I had done more than enough mother and father work and had put my childhood to bed. Well, I still had two books worth of work to do!—*The Resurrection of the Unicorn* on working through my mother complex, and *The Father Quest*, my journey into understanding this great archetypal figure.

Experiences and associations with our personal parents, or the lack or loss of parents, cluster around an archetype and become complexes. Our father complexes have at their core the Great Father or God archetype. In my book, *The Father Quest*, I designate our personal fathers by writing the word "father" in lower case. When I refer to the archetype of FATHER I write it in all capital letters to show that it is an image from the collective unconscious, the realm in our psyche that is much greater than our personal experience, knowledge, and understanding.

Our mother complexes have their core in the Great Mother or Goddess archetype. The energy fields of these two great archetypes are the biggest dynamos that drive our personalities. Our relationship to these energy fields can fill us with confidence, purpose, and enthusiasm or with hopelessness and despair.

Bonding, the lack of bonding, or having a destructive relationship with our personal parents generates the complexes (i.e., the psychic energy fields that will color our entire relationship to life). Let me share with you a few opening pages of Chapter Five in my book, *The Father Quest*, that addresses how these relationships develop:

> Since the beginning of our kind, the image of the mother cradling her infant has symbolized the state of inner harmony. The foundation of our psychological relationship to life rests on our personal experience of this metaphor as infants. We carry this experience, in Erikson's terms "trust versus mistrust," straight into adulthood. It is the job of the Fathers to provide the

emotional safety for mothers and children that insures the development of this image of trust in life. As we grow, we can then internalize this image as a basis for our development and self-actualization. If we have developed a sense of trust in ourselves and life, we are much less vulnerable to becoming overly dependent on other people, outer objects and situations, such as spouses, institutions, and conventional values.

Today we live in a world where our children are scared. Our inner unity and security is split. We are over-involved in the demands of outer worlds at the expense of our inner lives. We are so alienated from our own natures that we have practically forgotten that they even exist. Mother and child, as a metaphor or a concrete reality are not safe in our world. The Fathers have failed in their most elementary task.

For several generations now, the expectant father in our culture has been portrayed in the media as an awkward, bumbling figure who can do little but get in the way. In the last few decades, men have become more actively involved in the birth process, coaching their wives through labor, and being present at the birth. But even though the involved father is an improvement on the buffoon pacing in the waiting room, and even though maternal men can sometimes be helpful and may make better mothers than their wives—is it appropriate that fathers take on the role of mothering? Should fathers become nurturing duplicates of mothers? Joseph Campbell, when speaking of males, began by discussing Jane Goodall's chimps:

*...males control an area some thirty miles in circumference, and they know where the bananas are. When the bananas are failing in one area, they know where to go for more. They also are defenders. They defend against invasion by other tribes.*

*And just in the primary way, the function of the*

*male in this society is to prepare and maintain a field within which the female can bring forth the future.*

The child psychiatrist D. W. Winnicott maintains that the appropriate role of the father is similar to the natural role of male chimps—to provide a "protective covering" for the mother so that she can turn her full attention to bearing and nurturing the baby. Early infancy, when the world of the family begins imprinting itself on the infant's psyche, is a critical time in our emotional development. And much of the infant's view of the world is filtered through the mother's body and the emotional attitudes her body reflects. A mother who is nervous, anxious, or resentful of the birth will lead her child to feel out of adjustment psychologically. This child will have a personality founded on a deep sense of anxiety and mistrust in the world.

A mother who is sufficiently gentle, loving, and emotionally secure (Winnicott calls this the "good enough mother," in order to counteract the illusion that mothers must be perfect) will help her infant develop a basic sense of trust in life and in their place in the world. Winnicott maintains that it is the father's role to provide the mother with the peace she needs to be a "good enough mother."

Of course, this greatly oversimplifies the situation. Life is complex, and the mother-infant relationship can be disturbed for any number of reasons, early deaths, illnesses, separations, or deprivations due to a myriad of crises. Also declaring mothers responsible for the relationship's success or failure is much too easy an answer. My point is that fathers, and the cultural Fathers, play an important part in this primary relationship.

Even though we are not chimps, with a need to defend our territory from intruders, we still need to defend our family (and ourselves) from fear. From a psychological perspective, the wounding of the feminine in our culture has led many mothers to mistrust the world and men to a greater degree than ever before, and this mistrust has affected our children. Also, we live in a fearful society. The *Atlantic Monthly* recently ran a lead article entitled "Growing Up Scared" that showed how all of our children in every socioeconomic level live with fear every day. Furthermore, we have created an economic system that requires both parents to work in many cases, almost guaranteeing stress for young parents. Finally, as human beings, our primary sense of security often comes from caring, trust, and emotional closeness, and our sense of community and family is very strained. The threats to parenting are more complicated and serious than ever. It is the Father's responsibility to consciously face them in order to create a safe society and a protective covering "to bring forth the future."

## Father and Mother

As a baby emerges from the period of complete dependence on the mother, it becomes conscious of the father not just as a familiar figure, but as a figure who is also different from the mother. The presence of this additional parent reduces stress for both the mother and the child and adds balance and stability to the family in a healthy situation.

As children continue to grow, they get to know their fathers as individuals and so learn more about a real relationship that includes love and respect. For his part, the father should let his children see enough of his real self over the years to demystify himself so that his children can relate to him as a human being, not as a god or distant figurehead. If so, a father can open up a whole new perspective on life for his children. When he joins them in play or takes them out, he adds valuable new elements to their experience and helps them see the world through a new pair of eyes.

As the father begins to have an influence on his child, he activates an archetypal pattern whose nature is opposed to that of the mother's. In elemental terms, the FATHER represents doing and the MOTHER represents being. This FATHER archetype determines our relationship to society, to reason, and to the spirit and the dynamism of nature. The actual father carries this archetypal image in the life of the child, just as the actual mother carries the archetypal image of the MOTHER.

It's vitally important to distinguish between the archetypes and actual fathers and mothers when we talk about a father helping a child "separate from the mother." What we mean is that in order to become adults, we must separate from our own dependency needs represented by the archetypal image of the MOTHER. This separation from the MOTHER doesn't necessarily mean alienation from your real mother unless perhaps she refuses to participate in the process of psychological maturation. And even while a father is helping his son separate from the MOTHER, he must support the real mother emotionally during the period of separation.

Psychological growth involves separating the archetypal images from the real parents and integrating them into our own personalities. This procedure happens on three levels. First, we separate from our mothers, then from our fathers, and then the world or cultural parents—the guiding social conventions of our time that can entrap us in societal obligations.

This process can take years and, if it goes reasonably well, it gives us the opportunity to have a genuine relationship with both our parents and our own children. If the process goes poorly, usually because the parents fight against it in some way, then all parties are likely to wind up angry and resentful, or else dependent on or alienated from one another.

Many of my analysands are haunted by the commandment, "Honor your father and mother." They end up wracked with guilt and shame because they feel they should "honor" a parent who intimidated and brutalized them through their entire childhood. In reality, they dislike or even hate their parents, but they torture themselves thinking they should be able to forgive their parents because they "did the best they could." (The fact is, if someone has abused you, it is simply healthier and more human to entirely distance yourself from them.)

To honor your father and mother psychologically means to be conscious of the images they have left within our personalities and of the power those images have to shape our destinies. We must honor these images or be victimized by them. Once we have become an individual and have differentiated from our parents, and our parental complexes, these inner parental images become archetypal companions, like the wise old man or the wise old woman, and bless us with their special energy.

We can find an example of this process in the elder wisdom of mythology. In Book Sixteen of *The Odyssey*, Telemachus and his father, Odysseus, are reunited by Athene. A very poignant passage outlines the process that enabled Telemachus to remove the godly (archetypal) image of his father and reconcile with the human being previously hidden by this representation of the godly image. When Odysseus is first revealed by Athene, Telemachus refuses to accept the identity of his father. He responds with fear that Odysseus is not his father, but some god deluding him to increase his pain and sufferings and beseeches him for mercy. Odysseus replied:

> *No god, why take me for a god? No, no. I am that father whom your boyhood lacked and suffered pain for lack of. I am he!*

Once again Telemachus rejected this possibility, saying:

> *...Meddling spirits conceived this trick to twist the knife in me...*

Odysseus then instructed him to bear the manhood he had earned and conduct himself like a prince. With this admonishment, Telemachus accepted Odysseus as his father and they embraced and wept.

> *...Telemachus began to weep. Salt tears rose from the wells of longing in both men, and cries burst from them as keen and fluttering as those of the great taloned hawk, whose nestlings farmers take before they fly. So helplessly they*

*cried, pouring out tears, and might have gone on weeping
until sundown...*

In this beautiful poetry we can experience the deep yearning
for, and the intense joy of, being able to reconcile with the humanity of a parent. The eternal truth in this scene reminds us that
Athene, the goddess of wisdom and courage, must mediate this
reconciliation. We also must note carefully Odysseus's example; for
it is the responsibility of the parent, specifically the father, to take
the initiative and insist upon giving up his larger-than-life image as
well as insisting on his son's bearing himself with maturity.

## Working with Parental Complexes

There are three important additional points I want to make now.
The first point is one that is rarely mentioned. Every mother and
father develops a son or daughter complex in relation to each of
their children. These complexes involve the expectations or lack
of expectations and disappointments they enclose the child in as
they grow. In my own case these expectations started before I was
born. These projections may change as children grow. And, if parents are unwilling to give up these complexes and projections, then
once their son or daughter wants their authenticity to be recognized, valued, and affirmed, an irreconcilable difference will come
between the parent and the son or daughter. You cannot reconcile
with someone who won't give up a complex that typecasts you into
a particular definition of identity.

Secondly, we must all separate from our mother and father
complexes. For this reason, the Jungian analyst Dr. Verena Kast refers to our complexes as the "originally" positive or negative mother
or father complex. Complexes can develop in many ways. However, if we are seeking authenticity and a life of our own, each of
them will eventually hold us hostage. Even a complex that has been
life-enhancing will later become a trap or prison if we don't separate from it. Of course, it is when it becomes a trap or prison that
we usually discover the complex.

Thirdly, it is a common misunderstanding with many psychologically minded people and even therapists that one can internalize the "good" image of the therapist in order to counter or replace the negative image of the parent in a negative mother or father complex. *This idea is not true.* The Jungian analyst Hans Dieckmann explores this situation in his book, *Complexes.* Plus, my own personal and professional experience validates this reality. The good image of the therapist can only at best cause the negative complex to recede into the unconscious from which it will later return, often with renewed strength. Complexes must be worked through and integrated.

And, a fourth point…as you know we live in what we refer to as a patriarchy. This means that our culture has a negative father complex. And this means that if we are unhappy, if life is bad or our self-esteem is low, we are compelled to think that achievement is the only thing that can help us. In this case, achievement is not fueled by the pleasure, love, or creativity in what we are doing. It is driven by compulsion. This compulsion can never be satisfied. (This achievement mentality has been developed out of all that is motherless and unfeminine and reflects the total lack of a positive father, a positive patriarchal influence in our culture.)

The emotional core of our personality complexes becomes activated when some powerful event, encounter, or demand touches an area that we once had trouble dealing with. Or, if our complex is strong enough it can become a general part of our world view or even color our entire worldview. When we are "in a complex," so to speak, we become rigid, anxious, and generally emotional. We will frequently defend ourselves by attacking, in stereotypical ways—meaning the same old patterns we have used many times. Complexes close us down, limit our ability to hear others, to grow, to imagine, and to consider new possibilities.

Complexes were originally formed in childhood but may surface at any age. In most cases, they result from the repeated interaction between child and parent or child and family. For example, at one point in Margaret's work, she recalled having an image or dream of her father when she was very young. In this image her father was a giant, dwarfing and terrifying her. Even thinking about this image made her want to shrink up and sink into the ground. She wondered if she had been sexually abused. The answer turned out to be no, not sexually abused, but emotionally violated and intimidated, which was reflected in the symbolic thinking of the child.

If, however, a complex results from one big trauma, it is usually abandonment. Loss, abuse, violence or some other catastrophic wound cause a certain kind of complex or wound to the personality that requires that we carefully bring the lost child back into consciousness in the safety of an analytic container. The theme of the abandoned child is archetypal and we all experience it in some ways. In dreams it may represent a complex where we have abandoned our future potentials. Harry Potter, as you know, was an orphaned child which can be experienced as abandonment, and touched this theme in both grown-ups and children.

---

## Questions to Expand Our Understanding

1. Once again we have covered a lot of intense material.
2. What kind of feelings or thoughts have come up in you?
3. Are they surprising?
4. I would also suggest you look over the chart:
   **Some General Characteristics of Parental Complexes**
   and see what characteristics you might want to add or subtract.

---

# Some General Characteristics of Parental Complexes

### Positive Mother Complex in Men
Initially feels comfortable in himself and life. Tends to expect life to recognize and take care of him, tries to conform to other's needs and expectations. If he fails, he feels rejected and abandoned. Difficulty committing to relationships. Becomes depressed and discouraged at mid-life. Creates a warm atmosphere.

### Positive Mother Complex in Women
Has a fundamental faith in life and the world. Remains mother-dependent. Finds safety in dependency to the point of making people angry at her (her children, for example). She may have depressive and body image issues.

Note: It is surprising to realize that a positive mother complex can be responsible for depressive tendencies, anxiety, and narcissistic tendencies such as illusions of grandeur and oversensitivity to others' opinions later in life. The problem is that when we have a strong parental image in one complex, we usually have a weak one in the other parental complex. In this case a weak father complex.

### Positive Father Complex in Men
Sees himself as competent. Has a rock-solid identity. Slow to change or be creative. Not at ease with independent women. Has an unconscious ideology of control to minimize risk, recognition, and acceptance.

### Positive Father Complex in Women
Sees men as more interesting. Friendly, but distant and cool toward women. Overvalues their erotic capacity and undervalues intellect and ability. Self-esteem depends on men because they aren't grounded in the feminine. Afraid to make decisions. Anxious and defined by male values, school, and work.

Note: A positive father complex helps us go into the world with confidence and the capacity to be aggressive. But it leaves us short in Eros and the ability to experience being.

### Negative Mother Complex in Women
Must make great efforts to have any hopes of their needs being met. Life is cold, the world is without love. One feels distrust, anxiety, and a sense of having no right to exist. Very difficult to face the fear underlying one's life. May compensate by acting as if afraid of nothing.

### Negative Mother Complex in Men
Often feels paralyzed, helpless, and guilty. Makes strenuous demands on themselves. Takes refuge in achievement and career. Never feels really alive. May feel a knot of pain in the stomach from a deep fear they cannot trust life.

Note: A negative mother complex leaves us feeling like we and the world are bad and threatening. We are ruled by a basic sense of fear, distrust, and that we are to blame. And we are afraid of our underlying rage. These feelings make the struggle with the complex, which needs to be very aggressive, difficult.

### Negative Father Complex in Men
The father, by upholding his rules, destroys the son's self-esteem. To rebel means to lose the father's blessing. To follow the father's path means to lose oneself. Carries self-critical and self-undermining attitude into relationships. Easily humiliated or made to feel insignificant. Retreats into silence as a defense.

### Negative Father Complex in Women
Feels incompetent, lonely, and unable to speak for herself in relationships or in work and careers. May overcompensate with achievement. Has rage toward mother. Her development as a woman is violated. Feels "not good for anything."

Note: Negative father complexes destroy self-esteem and leave men and women hard on themselves and others. There is an underlying sense of rage at the mother for not protecting. Whenever a parent is destructive to a child, mythology (Gaia, Zeus and Kronos, for example) shows that it is an archetypal obligation for the other parent to totally defend the child.

## Stepping Out of the Dead Skin of Our Old Life

I want to invite you into a more relaxing change of pace. We are going to read a story, the Grimms' fairytale known as "The Donkey" or, as it is called in other versions, "Donkey Skin."

This story reminds us that we may grow up so identified with the values of our parents and society that our real selves are buried beneath the skin we developed that represents our parents' kingdom. A child who has not been mirrored by its mother and father, not permitted to think its own thoughts or feel its own feelings, has been forced symbolically to obey an outer and inner king and queen. The child's sense of inner authority fails to develop adequately, and focuses instead on "What will people think? What do people expect? What is the appropriate thing to do?" Destructive as this outer authority can be to our creativity and authenticity, it may force us to grow a defensive skin or persona to hide and protect who we really are. Our re-emergence depends upon our willingness to journey to another kingdom. Now I will invite you to sit back, relax and listen to the story.

### The Donkey

*Once upon a time there lived a King and a Queen, who were rich, and had everything they wanted, but no children. The Queen lamented over this day and night, and said: "I am like a field on which nothing grows." At last, God gave the Queen her wish, but when the child came into the world, it did not look like a human child, but was a little donkey. When the mother saw that, her lamentations and outcries began in real earnest; she said she would far rather have had no child at all than have a donkey, and that they were to throw it into the water that the fishes might devour it. But the King said: "No, since God has sent him he shall be my son and heir, and after my death sit on the royal throne, and wear the kingly crown." The donkey, therefore, was brought up and grew bigger, and his ears grew up high and straight.*

*And he was of a merry disposition, jumped about, played and took especial pleasure in music, so that he went to a celebrated musician and said: "Teach me your art, that I may play the lute as well as you do." "Ah, dear little master," answered the musician, "that would come very hard to you, your fingers are not quite suited to it, and are far too big. I am afraid the strings would not last." But no excuses were of any use—the donkey was determined to play the lute. And since he was persevering and industrious, he at last learnt to do it as well as the master himself.*

*The young lordling once went out walking full of thought and came to a well; he looked into it and in the mirror-clear water saw his donkey's form. He was so distressed about it, that he went into the wide world, and only took with him one faithful companion. They traveled up and down, and at last came into a kingdom where an old King reigned who had a single but wonderfully beautiful daughter. The donkey said: "Here we will stay," knocked at the gate, and cried: "A guest is without—open, that he may enter." When the gate was not opened, he sat down, took his lute and played it in the most delightful manner with his two fore-feet. Then the doorkeeper opened his eyes, and gaped, and ran to the King and said: "Outside by the gate sits a young donkey which plays the lute as well as an experienced master!" "Then let the musician come to me," said the King. But when the donkey came in, everyone began to laugh at the lute-player. And when the donkey was asked to sit down and eat with the servants, he was unwilling, and said: "I am no common stable-ass, I am a noble one." Then they said: "If that is what you are, seat yourself with the soldiers." "No," said he, "I will sit by the King." The King smiled, and said good-humoredly: "Yes, it shall be as you will, little ass, come here to me." Then he asked: "Little ass, how does my daughter please you?" The donkey turned his head towards her, looked at her, nodded and said: "I like her above measure, I have never yet seen anyone so beautiful as she is." "Well, then, you shall sit next her too," said the King. "That is exactly what I wish," said the donkey, and he placed himself by her side, ate and drank, and knew how to behave himself daintily and cleanly.*

*When the noble beast had stayed a long time at the King's court, he thought: "What good does all this do me, I shall still have to go home again," let his head hang sadly and went to the King and asked for his dismissal. But the King had grown fond of him, and said: "Little ass, what ails you? You look as sour as a jug of vinegar, I will give you what you want. Do you want gold?" "No," said the donkey, and shook his head. "Do you want jewels and rich dress?" "No." "Do you wish for half my kingdom?" "Indeed, no." Then said the King: "If I did but know what would make you content. Will you have my pretty daughter to wife?" "Ah, yes," said the ass, "I should indeed like her," and all at once he became quite merry and full of happiness, for that was exactly what he was wishing for.*

*So a great and splendid wedding was held. In the evening, when the bride and bridegroom were led into their bedroom, the King wanted to know if the ass would behave well, and ordered a servant to hide himself there. When they were both within, the bridegroom bolted the door, looked around, and as he believed that they were quite alone, he suddenly threw off his ass's skin, and stood there in the form of a handsome royal youth. "Now," said he, "you see who I am, and see also that I am not unworthy of you." Then the bride was glad, and kissed him, and loved him dearly. When morning came, he jumped up, put his animal's skin on again, and no one could have guessed what kind of a form was hidden beneath it. Soon came the old King. "Ah," cried he, "so the little ass is already up!*

*But surely you are sad," said he to his daughter, "that you have not got a proper man for your husband?" "Oh, no, dear father, I love him as well as if he were the handsomest in the world, and I will keep him as long as I live." The King was surprised, but the servant who had concealed himself came and revealed everything to him. The King said: "That cannot be true." "Then watch yourself the next night, and you will see it with your own eyes; and hark you, lord King, if you were to take his skin away and throw it in the fire, he would be forced to show himself in his true shape."*

*"Your advice is good," said the King, and at night when they were asleep, he stole in, and when he got to the bed he saw by the light of the moon a noble-looking youth lying there, and the skin lay stretched on the ground. So he took it away, and had a great fire lighted outside, and threw the skin into it, and remained by it himself until it was all burnt to ashes. But since he was anxious to know how the robbed man would behave himself, he stayed awake the whole night and watched. When the youth had slept his fill, he got up by the first light of morning, and wanted to put on the ass's skin, but it was not to be found. At this he was alarmed, and, full of grief and anxiety, said: "Now I shall have to contrive to escape." But when he went out, there stood the King, who said: "My son, whither away in such haste? What have you in mind? Stay here, you are such a handsome man, you shall not go away from me. I will now give you half my kingdom, and after my death you shall have the whole of it." "Then I hope that what begins so well may end well, and I will stay with you," said the youth. And the old man gave him half the kingdom, and in a year's time, when he died, the youth had the whole, and after the death of his father he had another kingdom as well, and lived in all magnificence.*

---

### Questions to Expand Us:

1. As you are thinking about the story, write down the images that affected you the most.

2. Now I would like for you to reflect for a few more minutes and write down the feelings, ideas and questions the story brought up in you. I have another question for you to reflect on and write about.

3. How did this story remind you of parts of your own journey or struggles?

---

## The Journey of Initiation

Stepping out of the skins of our old selves is an interesting image. It takes courage. In primitive initiation ceremonies the initiates went through ordeals that were meant to separate them from their parents and families so they could become self-responsible members of the tribe with no more allegiances to their families. They were put through frightening ordeals that symbolized the death to the old and rebirth into the new. In initiations, one experienced the fear of death and of being in the liminal space, the space of betwixt and between death and rebirth, when the outcome is not known for sure.

Transformation is the same as initiation. The Jungian analyst Joseph Henderson adds that the fear of death is about "fear of change, or fear of growing up, or fear of becoming independent of the claims of the material world, or a mixture of all three." Whenever we take on the integration of a parental complex it will transform us, and somewhere in this process we will be afraid.

---

### Questions for Reflection

Think about what I have just said.

1. What are the benefits of this journey of initiation? What makes this process worthwhile? (a sense of well-being, freedom, being more alive)

2. Can it affect the body? (e.g., release pain or improve chronic pain, illness, cancer, weight, asthma, chronic fatigue)

---

## Facing the Complex and Transforming It

Now we are going to listen to another story. Some of you may be familiar with it. We used it in our book, *Like Gold Through Fire*, and it comes from the book *The Great Divorce* by C. S. Lewis. By this time I'm sure that many of you have become aware that strangely enough, we actually like some of our complexes. I enjoyed my fascination with Porsches. A central complex or complexes will color the nature of our identity and how we react to the world like pouring dark red wine into water. In many cases we will begin to say, "This is just who I am," and turn the defense of the complex into a defense of who we are. Then we are living as a ghost of who we really could be. Now let's see what happens in our story...

### *The Great Divorce by C. S. Lewis*

*I saw coming towards us a Ghost who carried something on his shoulder. Like all the Ghosts, he was unsubstantial, but they differed from one another as smokes differ. Some had been whitish; this one was dark and oily. What sat on his shoulder was a little red lizard, and it was twitching its tail like a whip and whispering things in his ear. As we caught sight of him he turned his head to the reptile with a snarl of impatience. "Shut up, I tell you!" he said. It wagged its tail and continued to whisper to him. He ceased snarling, and presently began to smile. Then he turned and started to limp westward, away from the mountains.*

*"Off so soon?" said a voice.*

*The speaker was more or less human in shape but larger than a man, and so bright that I could hardly look at him. His presence smote on my eyes and on my body too (for there was heat coming from him as well as light) like the morning sun at the beginning of a tyrannous summer day.*

*"Yes. I'm off," said the Ghost. "Thanks for all your hospitality. But it's no good, you see. I told this little chap," (here he indicated the Lizard), "that he'd have to be quiet if he came—which he insisted on doing. Of course his stuff won't do here: I realize that. But he won't stop. I shall just have to go home."*

*"Would you like me to make him quiet?" said the flaming Spirit— an angel, as I now understood.*

*"Of course I would," said the Ghost. "Then I will kill him," said the Angel, taking a step forward.*

*"Oh-ah-look out! You're burning me. Keep away," said the Ghost, retreating.*

*"Don't you want him killed?"*

*"You didn't say anything about killing him at first. I hardly meant to bother you with anything so drastic as that."*

*"It's the only way," said the Angel, whose burning hands were now very close to the Lizard.*

*"Shall I kill it?"*

*"Well, that's a further question. I'm quite open to consider it, but it's a new point, isn't it? I mean, for the moment I was only thinking about silencing it because up here—well, it's so damned embarrassing."*

*"May I kill it?"*

*"Honestly, I don't think there's the slightest necessity for that. I'm sure I shall be able to keep it in order now. I think the gradual process would be far better than killing it."*

*"The gradual process is of no use at all."*

*"Don't you think so? Well, I'll think over what you've said very carefully. I honestly will. In fact I'd let you kill it now, but as a matter of fact I'm not feeling frightfully well today. It would be silly to do it now. I'd need to be in good health for the operation. Some other day, perhaps."*

*"There is no other day. All days are present now."*

*"Get back! You're burning me. How can I tell you to kill it? You'd kill me if you did."*

*"It is not so."*

*"Why, you're hurting me now."*

*"I never said it wouldn't hurt you. I said it wouldn't kill you."*

*"Oh, I know. You think I'm a coward. But it isn't that. Really it isn't. I say! Let me run back by tonight's bus and get an opinion from my own doctor. I'll come again the first moment I can."*

*"This moment contains all moments."*

*"Why are you torturing me? You are jeering at me. How can I let you tear me to pieces? If you wanted to help me, why didn't you kill the damned thing without asking me— before I knew? It would be all over by now if you had."*

*"I cannot kill it against your will. It is impossible. Have I your permission?"*

*The Angel's hands were almost closed on the Lizard, but not quite. Then the Lizard began chattering to the Ghost so loud that even I could hear what it was saying.*

*"Be careful," it said. "He can do what he says. He can kill me. One fatal word from you and he will! Then you'll be without me for ever and ever. It's not natural. How could you live? You'd be only a sort of ghost, not a real man as you are now. He doesn't understand. He's only a cold, bloodless abstract thing. It may be natural for him, but it isn't for us. Yes, yes. I know there are no real pleasures now, only dreams.*

*But aren't they better than nothing? And I'll be so good. I admit I've sometimes gone too far in the past, but I promise I won't do it again. I'll give you nothing but really nice dreams—all sweet and fresh and almost innocent. You might say, quite innocent."*

*"Have I your permission?" said the Angel to the Ghost.*

*"I know it will kill me."*

*"It won't. But supposing it did?"*

*"You're right. It would be better to be dead than to live with this creature."*

*"Then may I?"*

*"Damn and blast you! Go on can't you? Get it over. Do what you like," bellowed the Ghost: but ended, whimpering, "God help me. God help me."*

*Next moment the Ghost gave a scream of agony such as I never heard on Earth. The burning One closed his crimson grip on the reptile: twisted it, while it bit and writhed, and then flung it, broken backed, on the turf.*

*"Ow! That's done for me," gasped the Ghost, reeling backwards.*

*For a moment I could make out nothing distinctly. Then I saw, between me and the nearest bush, unmistakably solid but growing every moment solider, the upper arm and the shoulder of a man. Then brighter still and stronger, the legs and hands. The neck and golden head materialized while I watched, and if my attention had not wavered I should have seen the actual completing of a man—an immense man, naked, not much smaller than the Angel. What distracted me was the fact that at the same moment something seemed to be happening to the Lizard. At first I thought the operation had failed. So far from dying, the creature was still struggling and even growing bigger as it struggled. And as it grew, it changed. Its hinder parts grew rounder. The tail, still flickering, became a tail of hair that flickered between huge and glossy buttocks. Suddenly I started back, rubbing my eyes. What stood before me was the greatest stallion I have ever seen, silvery white but with mane and tail of gold. It was smooth and shining, rippled with swells of flesh and muscle, whinnying and stamping with its hoofs. At each stamp the land shook and the trees dwindled.*

*The new-made man turned and clapped the new horse's neck. It nosed his bright body. Horse and master breathed each into the other's nostrils. The man turned from it, flung himself at the feet of the Burning One, and embraced them. When he rose I thought his face shone with tears, but it may have been only the liquid love and brightness (one cannot distinguish them in that country) which flowed from him. I had not long to think about it. In joyous haste the young man leaped upon the horse's back. Turning in his seat he waved a farewell, then nudged the stallion with his heels. They were off before I well knew what was happening. There was riding if you like! I came out as quickly as I could from among the bushes to follow them with my eyes; but already they were only like a shooting star far off on the green plain, and soon among the foothills of the mountains. Then, still like a star, I saw them winding up, scaling what seemed impossible steeps, and quicker every moment, till near the dim brow of the landscape, so high that I must strain my neck to see them, they vanished, bright themselves, into the rose-brightness of that everlasting morning.*

Now I would like for you to make this story more personal. If you wish, go back and read the story again slowly.

1. What kind of thoughts and feelings came up in you about the Ghost? What might the Ghost symbolize? What might it be like to live in an insubstantial body? What do you know of the Ghost within yourself? Take a few minutes to write this for yourself.

2. What more can you say about the Lizard? What might the Lizard symbolize? Why might the Lizard want to keep the Ghost in a dream or unconscious state? How does the Lizard help keep the Ghost in an insubstantial state of being? Take a few minutes to write how you know the Lizard within yourself.

3. What do you know of "the gradual process" and other delays and excuses in your life as you try to avoid transformation and "keep it in order"? What are ways we try to keep

our children in "the gradual process"? In what ways does our culture encourage "the gradual process" and avoidance of transformation?

4. The Lizard is transformed into a horse. What might the horse symbolize? What do you know of the horse energy in you? What might be keeping the Lizard in you from being transformed into a beautiful horse?

---

### Questions to Expand Our Understanding

1. How do the man and the horse relate to each other?

2. What do you think about the angel? What might the angel symbolize? How might you know when the angel is near you? Can you see this story within you now?

---

## Quotations for Reflection

*Now, in order to help us explore growth, transformation, and complexes further, read each quotation. Then, after each quotation, take five minutes to write your reflections:*

**QUOTATION 1:** "A narrow, defensive, threatened ego will refuse the complexes entrance, deny their existence and repress their energy. Thus the complexes come to thrive and grow stronger in the darkness of the shadow. They cannot, then, travel their customary route from archetypal territory into the terra firma of the ego... Just imagine the truck drivers who have come from faraway lands, have had to travel over those 'inconvenient and steep footpaths,' now waiting outside the city gates of ego-consciousness to unload their diverse and complex merchandise, but not let in. They will soon grow impatient, irritated and angry. If unrelated to, they might possibly become violent, as the soul-food they are bringing is spoiled, having incubated for too long in the womb of the shadow."

**QUOTATION 2:** "'Honor your father and mother' is a commandment that damages us greatly according to the well-known child psychologist Alice Miller in her book *The Body Never Lies.* Her point is that this commandment has become so literal and so ingrained in our social system of moral values that it causes us to automatically repress our feelings about our parents, blame ourselves for their failures and seek to forgive and reconcile rather than seek out the truth of our own experiences. From a Jungian position this cultural attitude makes us feel we are judging them rather than searching for the truth of our own reality."

**QUOTATION 3:** "If we need to cure, fight, defeat, overcome, or even correct a complex we have made it into an enemy and are losing the value in it. Of course, this kind of thinking is counter-cultural. It negates our ideas of control, rationality, curing and to some extent alleviating human misery. But, if we take the Jungian position of accepting it, which doesn't mean embracing it, we immediately gain some distance from it which opens many doors as to how to relate to it."

**QUOTATION 4:** "In individuation we ground ourselves in the part of the feminine, *Eros,* that is relational and feeling, that comes from the heart. And, we learn that our inner relationships are the foundation for our outer ones, as well as our relationship to life and the Divine. It is how we accept ourselves, find the courage to sacrifice our self-images again and again in order to relate to our complexes and find the promise of an enlarged life that actually frees us from our past and self-defeating habits."

---

### Questions to Expand Our Understanding

As we conclude, there are several additional questions I would like to ask you:

1. What surprised you the most about this experience?
2. What moved or inspired you the most?

---

In closing, I would like to say that whenever we choose to work through a complex, we are transforming a force that has been diminishing us…that has been contributing to our feelings of smallness, impotence, and helplessness. The result is that we have less need to feel powerful, inflated, and superior or to take refuge in idealism and formality. Let us make this choice because it opens us to the fullest experiences of life and love.

# RESOURCES

## C. G. Jung Resources

Jung, C. G. (1954) *The Collected Works*. Trans. by R. F. C. Hull and ed. by H. Read, M. Fordham, G. Adler, and W. McGuire. Bollingen Series XX (vols. 2, 5, 7, 8, 9, 10, 11, 18) Princeton: Princeton University Press.

————. *Studies in Word Association*. (Vol. 2)

————. *Symbols of Transformation*. (Vol. 5)

————. *The Relations between the Ego and the Unconscious*. (Vol. 7)

————. *The Structure and Dynamics of the Psyche*. (Vol. 8)

————. *A Review of the Complex Theory*. (Vol. 8)

————. *Psychological Aspects of the Mother Archetype*. (Vol. 9i)

————. *The Spiritual Problem of Modern Man; The Undiscovered Self. Civilization in Transition*. (Vol. 10)

————. Psychotherapists or the Clergy; Answer to Job. *Religion: West and East* (Vol. 11)

————. Commentary on *The Secret of the Golden Flower*. Alchemical Studies. (Vol. 13)

————. Rex and Regina. *Mysterium Coniunctionis*. (Vol. 14)

————. The Tavistock Lectures; The Symbolic Life; Adaptation, Individuation, Collectivity. *The Symbolic Life*. (Vol. 18)

————. (1933) *Modern Man in Search of a Soul*. Trans. by W. S. Dell and Cary F. Baynes. New York: Harcourt, Brace and Company

————. (1961) *Memories, Dreams, Reflections*. Recorded and edited by A. Jaffe. New York: Vintage

————. (1964) (Conceived and edited.) *Man and His Symbols*. New York: Doubleday

————. (1976) *C. G. Jung Letters, Vol. I and II*. London: Routledge and Kegan

————. (1988) *Nietzsche's Zarathustra: Notes on the Seminar in 1934-1939*. Princeton: Bollingen Series

## General Resources

Campbell, J. (1968) *The Hero with a Thousand Faces*. New York: Princeton

———. ed. (1968) *The Mystic Vision: Papers from the Eranos Yearbooks*. Princeton: Princeton University Press

———. (1990) *Transformation of Myth Through Time*. New York: Harper & Row

Davies, Robertson. (1996) *The Merry Heart: Reflections on Reading, Writing and the World of Books*. New York: Penguin

De Castillejo, I. C. (1973) *Knowing Woman*. New York: Putnam

Dieckmann, H. (1999) *Complexes: Diagnosis and Therapy in Analytical Psychology*. Trans. by Boris Mathews. Evanston: Chiron

Edinger, E. (1972) *Ego and Archetype*. New York: Penguin Books

———. (1984) *The Creation of Consciousness: Jung's Myth for Modern Man*. Toronto: Inner City

Eliade, M. (1958) *Rites and Symbols of Initiation*. New York: Harper & Row, Torch Books

———. (1987) *Encyclopedia of Religion*. New York: MacMillan

Fromm, E. (1995) *The Essential Fromm: Life Between Having and Being*. ed. R. Funk. New York: Continuum

Harris, B. (2002) *Sacred Selfishness: A Guide to Living a Life of Substance*. San Francisco: New World Library

———. (2007) *The Fire and the Rose: The Wedding of Spirituality and Sexuality*. Evanston: Chiron

Hillman, J. (1967). *Insearch: Psychology and Religion*. Dallas Spring Publications

Huxley, A. *The Perennial Philosophy: An Interpretation of the Great Mystics, East and West*. New York: Harper Collins

Jacobi, J. (1971) *Complex/Archetype/Symbol*. New York: Bollingen

Jaffe, A. (1984) *The Myth of Meaning in the Work of C. G. Jung*. Zurich: Daimon

Johnson, Robert A. (1986) *Inner Work: Using Dreams and Active Imagination for Personal Growth*. San Francisco: Harper and Row

Kast, V. (1977) *Father/Daughter, Mother/Son*. Rockport: Elements.

Lewis, T., F. Amin, R. Lannon. (2000) *A General Theory of Love*. New York: Vintage

Luke, H. M. (1988) *The Voice Within: Love and Virtue in the Age of the Spirit*. New York: Crossroads

Mattoon, M. (1981*) Jungian Psychology in Perspective*. New York: The Free Press

Neumann, E. (1944) *The Origins and History of Consciousness*. Trans. by Ralph Mannheim. New York: Pantheon

Neumann, N. (1989) *The Place of Creation*. Princeton: Princeton University Press

Paz, O. (1990) *The Other Voice: Essays on Modern Poetry*. Trans. by H. Lane. New York: Harcourt

Rilke, R. M. (1975) *Rilke on Love and other Difficulties*. Trans. by J. J. L. Mood. New York: Norton

———. (1984) *Letters to a Young Poet*. Trans. by S. Mitchell. New York: Random House

Shalit, E. (2002) *The Complex: Path of Transformation from Archetype to Ego*. Toronto: Inner City

———. (2008) *Enemy, Cripple and Beggar: Shadows in the Hero's Path*. San Francisco: Fisher King

Underhill, E. (1999) *Mysticism: The Nature and Development of Spiritual Consciousness*. Oxford: One World Publications

Von Franz, Marie-Louise. (1978) *An Introduction to the Psychology of Fairy Tales*, 4th edition. Dallas, TX: Spring

Whitmont, E. G. (1969) *The Symbolic Quest: Basic Concepts of Analytical Psychology*. Princeton: Princeton University Press

Woodman, M., K. Danson, M. Hamilton, R. Allen. (1992) *Leaving My Father's House: A Journey to Conscious Femininity*. Boston: Shambala

# Author's Bio

 Bud Harris, Ph.D., as a Jungian analyst, writer, and lecturer, has dedicated his life to helping people grow through their challenges and life situations into becoming "the best versions of themselves." Bud originally became a businessman in the corporate world and then owned his own business. Though very successful, he began to search for a new version of himself and life when, at age 35, he became dissatisfied with his accomplishments in business and challenged by serious illness in his family. At this point, Bud returned to graduate school to become a psychotherapist. After earning his Ph.D. in psychology and practicing as a psychotherapist and psychologist, he experienced the call to further his growth and become a Jungian analyst. He then moved to Zurich, Switzerland where he trained for over five years and graduated from the C. G. Jung Institute. Bud is the author of thirteen informing and inspiring books. He writes and teaches with his wife, Jungian analyst, Massimilla Harris, Ph.D., and lectures widely. Bud and Massimilla both practice as Jungian analysts in Asheville, North Carolina. For more information about his practice and work, visit: www.budharris.com or https://www.facebook.com/BudHarrisPh.D.

# A Note of Thanks

Whether you received *Becoming Whole: A Jungian Guide to Individuation* as a gift, borrowed it from a friend or purchased it yourself, we're glad you read it. We think that Bud Harris is a refreshing, challenging and inspiring voice and we hope you will share this book and his thoughts with your family and friends. If you would like to learn more about Bud Harris, Ph.D. and his work, please visit: www.budharris.com or https://www.facebook.com/BudHarrisPh.D.